Crossing
THE
Caring Bridge:

What Death Taught Me About
Life, Love, Gratitude, and Grace

Jan Briddell Stevens

outskirts
press

This book is dedicated to all who have suffered the loss of a loved one…

To all who are facing the loss of a loved one…

Or…

To those who are facing Death right now…

Morituri te salutamus.

Author Acknowledgments

There are so many people to thank for their individual kindnesses that it would take another book to fill – what a blessing it is to write that statement alone.

Note: Some names have been changed to protect the privacy of certain persons

I would, however, like to thank some specific people who participated in making this book a reality. First, I would like to thank **CaringBridge.org** who provided the platform for suffering patients and their families to support each other, honor loved ones, and connect through difficult times. Next, I want to thank Laurie Anne McCoy for believing in me – you never gave up on this project! I also thank all those who read my manuscripts in their various forms, weighed in on cover designs, and waded through book titles ad nauseum: my daughter - Chelsea Scriven, daughter - Alexis Stevens, my son, Mac Baldwin – for making me laugh through it all, my sisters - Connie Briddell and Peggy O'Neill, and brothers - Kent and Dan Briddell, my cousin - John Hayden, my friends and fellow grief survivors - John Chickering, Sheila Grifo Fredericks, Jackie Nasca, New York Ink's Tattoo Tony

Rodriguez, and Ben Putnam, young son of renowned life coach, Jeff Putnam for agreeing to read and give feedback.

Thanks to MD firefighter/paramedic legend and friend, Skip Carey, for his never-flagging support, and to lifelong friend, Ellen Doherty Granoff, for the "girl get-a-ways" that always renewed my spirit. Special thanks to daughter, Heather Klatt, for our many heart-to-hearts about her dad so that we got it just right (and we did!). A deep felt thank you to longtime friend, musician, TV personality, and author, Daryl Davis, for teaching me how to sing the blues and for our meaningful conversations on the significance of Death in our lives. A heartfelt thanks to friend, Joe Beckman, who was the originator of the nickname "Morty" for Death after he heard about my dream - he was joking, but it stuck. A salute to mentor Ron Klein, master hypnotist, who helped me re-frame grief and loss. A hearty thanks to my Outskirts Press team including: publishing advisor, Jamie Belt, my editor, Terri Abstein, my author representative, Dana Nelson, and my brave copyeditor Reba Hilbert (who took on this project even though she too lost a loved one to brain cancer). Thank you Outskirts Press for all your patience and hard work on the project working with the design team who pulled it all together. Very poignantly I must add, a loving thanks to my husband, Alan, for selflessly encouraging me to write this story, even reading it for typos – all the while stating, "I know if I'd met Steve in this life we would've been good friends." Finally, highest thanks to BOB, who makes all things possible…you'll know what I mean when you read on…

Table of Contents

Part One:
The Uninvited Guest

Part Two:
The Original Caring Bridge Journal for Steve Calloway

Part III:
The Aftermath—Death Takes His Leave

Prologue

So, in my dream: we were sitting in rocking chairs on my patio at 45-degree angles to one another, and I had just served my guest a hot cup of Earl Grey tea—a favorite of mine from years ago. He took it from me somewhat awkwardly, causing the cup to rattle against the saucer, and I remembered thinking—where did I get this fancy china, anyway? He fumbled with the spoon as if he'd never handled one before and just balanced the whole thing midair, watching me, waiting, and I realized he was following my lead.

My mother had taught me many things growing up, some of which I forgot, some of which I ignored, and most of which I remembered because she was a kind and gracious woman. Therefore, I smiled warmly at my guest to put him at ease and demonstrated stirring my tea, setting down my spoon, and taking a sip. My supposition was right as he earnestly followed my example. He was doing well until he put the cup to his mouth. He opened and tilted it just as I had done, but it was at that moment that I realized he had no lips...he had no muscle...no face...My guest was a skeleton, and to my astonishment, he emptied the entire cup of Earl Grey down his inky black robe. Even greater than the loss of a perfect cup of Earl

Grey, I found it horrifying to be sitting knee to bony knee with the Grim Reaper himself—Monsieur Death—and yet there he was dabbing at his dark gauzy robe with a napkin clasped between skeletal fingers, while balancing the rattling cup in the other hand. His sickle was casually leaning against the sliding glass doors behind him, and he seemed flustered, very flustered.

"Oh no! I'm so sorry!" he stammered with fleshless teeth. "No one ever invites me to sit, and now I've made a mess!" Fussing about like C3PO from Star Wars, *he babbled, "I haven't socialized in so long that I forgot that everything runs right through me!" He stopped dabbing to look at me pleadingly, and somehow there was life in those empty eye sockets. I sat there agape, then suddenly, and much to my dismay, I burst out laughing. Instantly mortified—as I was trained better by my mother—I clapped my hand over my mouth as we both froze. He, with that ridiculous napkin poised in one hand, teacup in the other, and I, like the speak-no-evil monkey. Time and space collapsed upon each other, and it could have lasted an hour or a mere second, but at the next moment, he threw back his skull and started cackling uncontrollably, slapping his femur with the napkin hand.*

"As you can see, I have a drinking problem!" he choked out between hoots and slaps, and I joined in until tears ran down my cheeks, laughing at the absurdity of this moment. We finally settled down, catching our breath, sighing, only to start up again as soon as we made eye contact. It was a good laugh, a cleansing laugh, the kind that purges the soul—not unlike a good cry.

At last, he composed himself enough to say, "Thank you for making me laugh—no one ever laughs with me, or tells jokes, or even smiles when I am around. You see, I don't get invited to many parties," at which, God help me, I burst into helpless giggles once more. When our mirth subsided, he sighed and set down his cup with shaky hands, and I suddenly felt incredibly drawn to and at the same time sorry for this…this…creature, so I placed a hand on his bony shoulder and patted it as my mother might have done. He looked at my hand, then up at me and said, "I have a really tough job, you know. I am not a bad guy, and I don't do the, uh, CHOOSING, I just pick up the packages."

"I know," I replied, though I really didn't know about any of this, but I somehow wanted to encourage this being who apparently had the crummiest job on the planet. "I think you're probably pretty misunderstood; maybe you just need to work on your approach," I offered, "you know, introduce yourself a little better, work on your image so you're not such a shock when you show up—you ARE pretty intimidating, you have to admit." All the while I was marveling at the concept that HE himself did not do the killing.

"What do you suggest?" he asked, genuinely interested, as if his image issues never occurred to him.

I thought for a second and said, "I don't know…perhaps you should be wearing something a little more…friendly and normal…" Of course, that was a mere drop in the bucket when considering that he had no skin…but this was my dream and therefore not required to make perfect sense.

He nodded thoughtfully, then put up a bony finger. "How 'bout a name tag?!"

"A what?" I was confused.

"You know!" He was inspired. "I could get one of those red

and white ones like they give people at parties or seminars that say HELLO: My Name Is: DEATH!"

I was in all truth previously referring to his morbid black, gauzy robe and scythe accessory, not a mere name tag, but it was clear he was trying to think out of the box, and it was something. Keeping true to my mother's gracious manners, I eagerly encouraged him, nodding and smiling. "Well now, that's a start," I acknowledged, "but DEATH is kind of a scary name...don't you think?"

"Well, how about Morty?" he suggested shyly. "That's what my mom calls me."

Holy chihuahua! I thought. Death has a mother? I marveled at the concept, but I felt I had to keep up my support for some strange reason. "Okay, Morty it is. Well, good start, Morty, high five!" I raised my hand and we slapped palm to skeletal palm and...

Death's hand fell off.

I awoke with a jolt and knew what I had to do. I had waited a whole seven years to do it, and I had no more excuses that didn't sound like wimpy cop-outs. Death had come for tea in my dreams, and we had shared a belly laugh, after which I had severed his hand. I had to write this book, if not for me, for him... and for those of us he's taken and especially for those of us he's left behind.

You see, I had already met Morty on various occasions, and I will admit that I used to quake with terror at the mere mention of him. He had taken people I loved, young and old—some for no good reason and way before their season, and others after a respectable time—but always leaving a void in his wake. It stood to reason he didn't get many invites, but now I was seeing him and his whole routine with fresh eyes.

Perhaps he is feared, reviled, cursed, and avoided because we simply do not truly know him. Like any victim of stereotyping, we make assumptions and generalizations about someone we have not taken the time to get to know. It is easy to rage against anonymous and faceless people who cut us off on the highway, but if we were to learn more, we might discover they were racing to a loved one's bedside or to their only child's graduation after fixing a flat, praying they didn't miss the first walk ever for a diploma in their family's history. When we have a chance to chat with these "strangers" in line at the bank or at the grocery store, we might find out that we're not so different after all, that we often want the same things. Suddenly, our sweeping assumptions seem somewhat foolish or even downright WRONG.

That occurred to me when I awoke from this dream about Death. It was so strange, so surreal, so funny, bizarre, and ridiculous that it challenged me to take a second look. Up until this point, Death, to me, had been an inevitable and unavoidable truth—the elephant in the room…or more graphically, the turd in the punch bowl at the garden party of life. The awkward, distasteful, destructive thing that everyone skirts around, averts their eyes from, and pretends isn't there. But we cannot ignore it forever, because sooner or later the elephant will sit on the couch and crush it, or your guest will dip the ladle into your homemade punch—with disastrous results. So, to save your home and party, one must acknowledge and herd the elephant or dive in and fish out the turd.

Elephants and turds are part of nature and normal living. They each have their appropriate and appointed places. So, too, does Death. He is as natural as breathing—everyone breathes… and everyone dies. If you look at it philosophically, Death is the biggest unifier on the planet, and if personified, he's the most open-minded, non-judgmental, all-inclusive being who will visit every single person without invitation—God is polite enough to be invited. Like God, the Grim Reaper doesn't care what color you are, your financial status, how many friends you have on social media, for whom you voted, what you name your Higher Power, or how perfectly organized you are or are not. He just shows up when it is time…and we never know exactly when that will be.

I suspect some of you reading this book are doing so because you have been warned that Death is headed to your home or to the home of someone you love. You don't know the exact date he will arrive, but you know he's on his way, drawing near, or possibly standing on the threshold…and you just don't know how to receive him. You might even try or have tried barricading the door, escaping to another locale, diverting him with medical magic, praying or willing him away, but he's coming nonetheless. Or, perhaps he's already come, and you're standing there surrounded by the broken china of your heart, wondering what just happened.

In the end…and make no mistake, THE END WILL COME. We can view Death as an awful turd in our punch bowl of life, or maybe, just maybe we can prepare a little, change our paradigm from thinking Mr. Reaper is disgusting, and instead accept him as a natural part of living—a promised visitor who will come to call for each of us in his time. He can be the foulness that spoils everything, or he can be the guest we've always expected, and how we receive him will make all the difference. When he is treated with respect and dignity, Death can even be a gentleman. He can teach us things we never knew. He can reveal things within ourselves that had once lain hidden. He can even make us laugh, and through that truth, he can even be transformed into an unlikely ally.

I am speaking through hindsight though, because I never had the grace or strength of character to come up with this myself. I only learned how to re-frame that inevitable visitor by watching a true gentleman die. This man guarded against Death for a long while, even defied him and told him to come back another day, but eventually, the caller always returns for the appointed rendezvous, and the man was ready to meet him with dignity and grace. In so doing, he taught me, and thousands of others along the way, how to die well. This man was my late husband, Stephen C. Calloway—father, grandfather, son, friend, and mentor to the firefighter/paramedics and countless others who had the privilege to meet him and bear witness to his all-too-early appointment with Death.

Part One

The Uninvited Guest

Chapter One

Death Decides to Get Trip Insurance

Whenever I am not certain I am going to be able to make a journey I have planned for whatever reason, I buy the trip insurance. Most of the time I do not, but occasionally I will get a hunch that something might go awry, so I spend a few extra bucks to do it. Usually I've been right. Well, I am pretty sure Death is at least prescient, so I think when he pulled the card for his visit to the Calloway household, he got that gut feeling that he ought to buy some trip insurance.

It wasn't because he'd already come to my home, or to Steve's for that matter. The Reaper had visited before, gathering my father, grandmother, beloved aunts and uncles, friends, and cousins, and he came rather abruptly to drop in on Steve's mother the day before she was scheduled to return home from the hospital after a bout of pneumonia. One would think we'd be on a first-name basis or at least on speaking terms, but he was (even in those cases) a respectful guest, showing up later in my loved ones' lives when his presence wasn't quite such a surprise, leaving rather quickly even after we'd laid out the good china for him.

Death didn't take out trip insurance for us because of the fortitude of *my* character or the strength of *my* constitution. I was just average and had had my struggles with Lyme disease, chemical pneumonia, and other maladies that did not leave me a spectacular specimen of robust health. I might've even been easy pickings for him without the miracle of antibiotics. No, the Big D took out trip insurance when he drew the card for a strong 55-year-old firefighter/paramedic who was a former farmer and whose hobbies included boating, fishing, woodworking, serious gardening, and even basket-weaving while teaching himself history and physics along the way. His health screenings were disgustingly clean despite his penchant for cigars. If anything caught Big D's eye, I was sure it was gonna be those dang cigars. But no.

Steve and I had met later in life and had married after a rather brief courtship in December of 2004. We had wonderful grown kids from prior marriages, and everyone got along as well as could be expected with their busy lives. He and I got along great, never fighting, laughing a lot, going to shows, enjoying making a home, traveling to favorite spots, volunteering to host wounded soldiers at our home near the beach so they could get a break from their therapy at Walter Reed Military Hospital. I was a teacher, and he, well, I already told you.

He was also an instructor for the many continuing education classes for medical personnel in the region, making their required credit hours tolerable if not downright fun. He was folksy, funny, irreverent, kind to a fault, and self-effacing. He could calm the most anxious patient on his ambulance simply by saying in his deep, rich voice, "Now listen here, you promise me YOU won't panic until you see ME panic, okay?" They would instantly agree, and he would never show panic, no matter how dire their condition happened to be.

He was good to the young guys who were just getting started in their medical careers, spending countless hours tutoring them so they could pass their certification exams, and he would do endless kindnesses for me like rub my aching feet after a long day at school, or build me furniture, birdhouses, and frames for my portraits and paintings. I would try to reciprocate, but he always outworked and "out-kinded" me. When I would take him dinner in a basket at the firehouse during his shift, the other guys would laugh, saying we were like two silly kids, whereupon he proved them right by skipping gleefully out to my car to greet me no matter how grueling a shift he was having.

He was tall, lanky, but muscular and deceptively strong. Once we were moving a piano that we were donating to a church with help from a crew of young guys sent over by the pastor. The guys were struggling with the piano's weight, and Steve said, "Now look, you guys get on that end…and I'll just…" and then he grabbed the empty end and lifted it in the trailer—three young men on one end and Steve on the other. He liked to shock people that way…allowing them to think one thing, then always proving them wrong.

At a black-tie gala for my private school where several parents were discussing something intellectual at our table, one of the men turned to Steve and kindly but a bit condescendingly began to explain a scientific concept that they'd just been discussing (as if Steve needed a dumbed-down version). Steve listened, tilting his head thoughtfully, and replied, "Well, relativity and quantum mechanics can be said to contradict one another, but I have great hope in the attempts at unification if we can just solve the question of the elusive force of gravity." Jaws went slack around the table, because these poor folks at this black-tie fund-raiser didn't know that in addition to saving lives and accomplishing other acts of everyday heroism, this former pig farmer turned firefighter had an IQ of 157. Death knew it, though, and that's why he bought that trip insurance.

Chapter Two

Death Meets the Miracle Man

Death is sometimes in an all-fire hurry and swoops in during the night or during a car ride or while we are sitting at our desk in a skyscraper on the 97th floor. He has too many appointments for niceties, and for some reason, which I expect him to explain when he comes for me, he doesn't always adequately announce himself. That can be earth-shattering to anyone. That is the turd in the punch bowl or the sucker punch in the gut. It doesn't seem sporting or fair of him to do that, so he deserves being called a jerk or turd or worse; however, just as we often do not know the full story before jumping to conclusions, I am going to cut Death some slack here. If there is one thing I've learned in life, it is that we cannot know the big picture, only little bitty pieces, and to judge a whole puzzle by one or two little pieces would be foolish. That said, Death gets a pass for now for his unannounced visits, because, after all, he is only the pickup and delivery guy.

Truth be known, it really doesn't matter how much advanced notice we get from Death; there is always a point in the process when we are not ready for his arrival, but if we get to know him just a little from hearing about the experience from someone who's met him firsthand, then maybe we won't be so terrified to open the door when he knocks. Because I gave him so much credit for the whole job, I believed the Grim Reaper pulled a fast one in taking Steve's mother (and a few young people I deeply loved in my life) without prior notice. But I sensed he took his time with Steve—knowing he would have to woo him—mainly because Death must have sensed he'd met his match. What I didn't know was that while the extraction was in his grasp, the decision to collect someone in the first place was not.

When one finds oneself in a crisis, one's judgment can become clouded—forest for the trees kind of thing—but after some time and distance, one can gain clarity on things. In retrospect, I think Death began the "courtship of Janni's husband" in the summer of 2007, just two and a half years after Steve and I married. If I were a cynic—which I am not—I would be telling you I knew things were too good to last, too good to be true, but that's a crock. Things were great…but that's not why they didn't last. I don't know how I know that—I just do. Anyway, Herr Scythemaster didn't care that we were happy and settling into a nice cozy life together. He simply pulled another card and had a contract to fill, so without much fanfare, he stepped into our hot tub one night in July without asking, mostly because he knew he'd never be invited in.

"I can't stand it," groaned Steve, as he wiped the water from his eyes. We sat in the hot tub—an almost nightly ritual for an achy firefighter and his equally achy wife.

"Can't stand what?" I asked without opening my eyes, thinking he was merely pontificating about some issue of social injustice.

"The heat!" he exclaimed, then splashed his way out of the tub and grabbed a towel.

Now, this was unusual. Steve was part reptile, baking on the nearest hot surface whenever he could, loving the summer heat, outlasting anyone who ever stepped foot into our hot tub. He had just sat down, and I could see new beads of sweat defying the swipes from his towel. For him to complain about the heat, I was sure he was sick—a virus or fever—so I followed him out and proceeded to treat him as a flu patient.

"I don't have the flu," he complained, "just overheated and a little dizzy. Probably just have a bug or maybe I need to eat." After which he showered, ate, fell asleep on the couch. When he awoke the following day, he seemed back to normal. Death must've been simply testing the water.

A few days after, I noticed Steve rubbing his temples and I asked him about it. "Just a little headache, that's all. I'll take some aspirin." He did, and that was the end of it until the next headache.

"You okay?" I caught him massaging his head again. "You have another headache?"

"Yes, but it's no biggie. I think I have a few allergies from the yard…feels like my sinuses." Then we tried some over-the-counter antihistamines, decongestants, and pain relievers that seemed to do the trick.

A week or two later, "You ready to go to the club?" I asked, referring to our plans to meet friends at our little redneck yacht club. He said he was, but when we arrived at our boat, he promptly fell asleep. Now Steve was a good napper, and he had been pulling some extra shifts for a few guys at the firehouse, so I chalked it up to that, but apparently, the Big D was making his move.

As the days wore on and I prepared for a new school year, Steve took a few more naps and slept a little more than usual, which should have alerted me. But Steve is not one to complain, and he passed my concerns off as nothing, assuring me he was fine. What he *wasn't* telling me was that the headache was constant, and it was getting worse. The Reaper apparently had his foot in the door.

I recall reading about the concept of FLASHBULB moments in life…you know, the times where someone asks, "Where were you on 911 when the towers fell?" or "What were you doing when the earthquake hit?" Those moments where time stands still, and you can remember everything in photographic detail because what follows literally or figuratively shakes you up and rocks your world!

This was mine: I was in school on my lunch break and saw on my phone that Steve had called—unusual because he usually texted, knowing I couldn't answer a live call—so I called him back. I was completely unprepared for what happened next—a FLASHBULB moment where Big D was winding up for a sucker punch to the gut.

"Hi honey!" I exclaimed.

"I can't…am boat…no right…think not trees to make…"

BAM! The wind was knocked out of me. Someone else might have thought it was a joke that Steve was playing, but I knew better. My father had had several mini-strokes before he passed just a few years prior, and he had moments of what they call aphasia, where words come out, but they're all wrong or inappropriate to the speaker's intention. This sounded the same.

"Oh no, Steve, where ARE you?" I was instantly frantic.

"Going to place…"

"What place? Steve, you need a hospital NOW!" I cried, and he managed a yes, that was where he was headed. Then he hung up, and I could not get him to answer again. I was beside myself with panic. Was he at the boat, which was forty minutes away, or on his way? Was he driving? Was someone taking him? Would he make it? I called the yacht club and they said he wasn't there anymore, having left a while ago, so I banked on the hospital or home.

I raced into the headmaster's office, explained my emergency, and he sent me on my way, making me promise to update him on Steve's progress as he, too, thought the world of Steve.

My next call was to the local ER where Steve often takes his patients and where I have many friends. I was relieved to find out that he had, in fact, made it there and was waiting for me. The nurse seemed calm, so I foolishly assumed things must be okay, but my gut told me to hurry anyway. I don't remember how I got there or how many rules of the road I broke—I just ended up running in the ambulance entrance and straight into several nurses and docs who did *not* look relaxed. In fact, one nurse—whose husband used to work with Steve—had been crying, so I was unnerved when she pulled me aside.

"Where is he?" I gasped. Then I was gently informed that Steve had staggered in, saying he needed help and had collapsed. It looked like a massive stroke, she told me, but they needed to transport him to the regional medical center for better diagnostics and intervention. The paramedics from Steve's company were already there to take us. I ran into his room and he was conscious, clearly confused, but not so far gone that he couldn't grab me into a huge one-armed hug.

"Sawwy," he sobbed, slurring the word, and I immediately lost my composure too, telling him through my tears that there was nothing for which to be sorry and that they were going to fix him up, even though I had no reason to know or believe it.

At the regional medical center, they took Steve straight to MRI while I waited.

Looking back, I realize that when we are at least a bit prepared, our encounters with Mr. Reaper can be somewhat civil, but when we're resistant, avoidant, or in denial, things can get ugly…and it's not always his fault. Sometimes people do and say insensitive or downright bad things, and that's what happened next.

I was sitting nervously in the ICU waiting area, watching for Steve to be returned from radiology, when an unfamiliar fireman from another company came in and said, "Hi Jan, I am Fred. My wife is a nurse here and I just heard about Steve. I am so sorry." Ordinarily, I would've been grateful for any support at that moment, but what he said next made my head spin. "I heard they said it's a brain tumor?" He was fishing for more information.

"What?" I barked, confused. "No, it is a massive stroke, they said…" Then I wasn't so sure, and the room began to spin faster. I looked at the clock, the door, and back at the man, hoping something would end this moment. He must have realized his egregious error and with a sick half-smile of pity said, "Oh, well, uh, my mistake. Well, we will be praying for you." Then he got up, scurrying for the exit as fast as he could go.

Now, ladies and gentlemen, I was a first responder when Steve and I met, and since then have become an RN and worked in the ER at a large trauma center, and let me tell you, there is a little thing called HIPAA that basically states that no medical worker who is privy to ANY thing about a patient has ANY right to discuss it outside of his or her scope of work as that patient's caregiver—not even to one's spouse. That ICU nurse had told her firefighter husband about my husband's brain tumor, and even though he was concerned, that stranger had blurted it out to me! He basically kicked down my front door and dragged DEATH himself in by the collar before the neurologist had even had the chance to gently sit us down and introduce us properly.

When the good doctor did finally speak with us in Steve's room, he confirmed what I was now secretly fearing—a brain tumor—and it was apparently not just any brain tumor, but a glioblastoma multiforme, most likely Stage IV. I had heard about those, and I had remembered nothing good.

"Translation please…" I solemnly requested when the neuro-surgeon joined us as well.

"Basically, this form of brain tumor is always malignant and is, as of this date, 100 percent fatal." I held my breath while Steve sat suddenly wide-eyed and confused.

"Prognosis?" I sounded robotic.

"If not treated, he has approximately one month. If treated, and I would send him for surgery at the Duke Brain Tumor Center," where Ted Kennedy was subsequently treated, "then he might have a year or a little more. But they're doing excellent drug trials all the time, and my friend is the chief neurosurgeon there. Would you like me to make that call?"

The ping-pong ball was on my side of the table, and Big D must've been watching the volley with interest.

"Yes, make it," I declared definitively, to which Steve sat up and patted the surgeon on the shoulder and collapsed back on the bed. It was then that the neurosurgeon fully recognized Steve as the paramedic who had always taught his continuing emergency medicine classes at the hospital. He seemed suddenly stunned, then softened, taking Steve's hand.

"Oh, my friend." Did his voice just catch? "I am sorry this thing is happening to you."

"It's not," croaked Steve, whose speech had regained some clarity after copious amounts of steroids had reduced the swelling in his brain, "you just watch…God is going to heal me, and there is no time limit on my ticket. Don't count me out so quickly, Doc, and thank you for helping to heal me."

The doctor smiled enigmatically; I tried to smile too, proud that I had such a brave husband, while inside screaming in terror. Death was now in my LIVING room, and I don't recall having invited him inside yet. I didn't let Steve see how terrified I was as I supported him in his conviction that he was going to be one of the lucky ones, and I let him drift off to sleep believing that he had a miracle coming. I know now, the Specter of Doom was standing in the shadows of that room that night. I know that he is powerful and unavoidable...but I also now know that there are chinks in his armor, and that he has an Achilles' heel—HOPE—and I think HOPE caught him with an uppercut to the chin when he came face-to-face with Steve, the Miracle Man, Calloway.

I imagined that the Miracle Man's hope confounded him so much that Death reacted instead of acting, causing him to turn his frustrated killer instincts on me. He had no card with my name on it in his bony grasp, but I pictured him coming at me nonetheless, swinging his scythe of doubt, despair, and doom until I was gripping my chair in paralyzed panic, pleading with God, "What are we going to do?"

Fear began to engulf me from the floor up—a cold, visible black mist that swirled around me, threatening to squeeze the breath from my lungs and sense from my mind. I bet you're thinking me overly dramatic here, but I can assure you that was what this rise of panic was like. It was suffocating, forcing me to gasp for air. Just when I was about to go under, I willed my eyes ever so slightly toward my husband, the Miracle Man, quietly sleeping with a slight smile on his face, and prayed, "Oh God, help us please!"

Immediately the mist vanished, and I envisioned myself a small child standing at the knee of a powerful presence that I could only interpret as Jesus from the Bible stories of my childhood—His feet in sandals peeking from beneath the hem of the shining white garment. I saw an old-fashioned package wrapped in muslin and tied with twine in my hands, and I knew it was "my burden," my "heavy load," my cares and woes and sorrows all bundled together. Then I handed the bundle upward to Jesus, saying, "Here, I can't do this anymore. It's too much for me to hold."

Jesus tenderly lifted the bundle from my tiny hands, and I laid my little head on His knee while He stroked my hair and said, "Everything is fine now; go to sleep." And I did until the following morning when I awoke to see that the sun was shining, and the darkness of fear was gone. The Specter had left the room after missing his connection that day, because one simple man believed in miracles. It seems his faith had been enough for the both of us.

Chapter Three

Death Sits Ringside

Just because we got a reprieve that day did not mean Death was finished with Steve. No sir, Big D had pulled the card and had to finish the job, but it was clear to him that it would not be an easy one. He must have recalled the words of the great poet Dylan Thomas, who wrote, "Do not go gentle into that good night... Rage, rage against the dying of the light." Big D knew a fighter when he encountered one, but rage? No, rage was not the Miracle Man's MO, and that made things tricky. Determination and faith? Now those were far more dangerous and worthy opponents to the Knockout King's throw-down, and Steve Calloway seemed to possess both. Just how much of each, time would reveal. Death had a job to do, but this one could take some doing.

So, like any polite visitor, Death initially took a seat and decided to watch the show. Little did he know what a show it was going to be. I imagined Old Death musing to himself, "This man is tougher than I'd expected, but I am patient; however, the woman looks as if she could break. I wonder if her card will come up soon. I've seen this all too often before—a BOGO, a Two-fer, Groupon!" Of course, I made the naive assumption that this would please the Reaper, but I now know Death doesn't set the agenda—that is something we project onto him unfairly.

When the bell sounded ringside, and the call came from Duke that we were going to have one of the finest surgeons in the nation and leading neuro-oncology teams working on Steve, the Miracle Man came out of his corner swinging. He told anyone who would listen that God had already healed him and that anything they were doing medically was merely for research and the betterment of others. He astounded people with his unshakeable optimism, and the folks at the Robert Preston Tisch Brain Tumor Center at Duke University Medical Center were captivated by him. The audience was inconsequential as he shared his message of hope and positivity with everyone, encouraging patients and healers alike everywhere we went.

Even following brain surgery, during which my two brothers and their wives sat vigil with me, Steve made it his mission to make everyone laugh, and laugh they did. His optimism was so high off the charts that he was the first patient ever to walk out of the ICU for a full discharge just two days after brain surgery. He managed to strut, albeit gingerly, grinning ear to ear through a gauntlet of doctors, nurses, housekeepers, and staff who applauded and high-fived him as he left the unit. Tears in their eyes, waving, and cheering—these folks had been deeply touched in a mere two days by the Miracle Man, who had the gift of inspiring all who came into his presence. It was breathtaking—the only thing lacking to make it film-worthy was a soundtrack.

Upon departing, we were required to stay at the medical hotel across the street from the medical center, but it was a freedom of sorts. We took daily walks in the gardens, fed the ducks, and ate at the cafeteria, where Steve would encourage other patients with far lesser maladies, and he was soon asked to join his first clinical or medical drug trial. When the director finished explaining how it would perhaps not help Steve but rather future patients, Steve not only agreed to help, but he also decided to sign up for an unheard of NINE clinical studies in total. I tried to intervene, claiming that he needed rest.

"No," he reasoned, "I feel great. I am healed, remember? But they can use me to help others who haven't been healed yet." And he truly believed it. His doctors would thank him profusely, grateful for his cooperation, patting Steve on the shoulder, but all the while still somehow have that knowing look on their faces— the one that says NO ONE SURVIVES GLIOBLASTOMAS. Even so, they would all watch him walk out, gazing after him, wondering what is it about that man?

Steve's positivity, along with my prior heavenly blessing in the hospital, were so powerful that we simply found joy in every moment. We smiled at strangers, found love notes from God everywhere—on license plates, billboards, anonymous notes left for us, songs—why it was as if Heaven truly opened its gates and showered us with healing love. Our first waitress's name was Angel; a license plate on the car next to ours said "TRUST ME," or another time one read "IMTHATIM," or a billboard would say, "I LOVE YOU, GOD" and nothing else, etc. Steve even recovered enough to go back to work if there was another paramedic with him. He managed to save several lives with his giant fifty-two-staple scar running like a huge question mark down the side of his head, bald as a billiard, under the ever-present hat that the docs required him to wear.

I was lucky enough to return to school and thank all those in person who'd flooded us with cards, food, and tokens of healing. The treatment complete, the tumor resected or "debulked" as the surgeons said, Steve's scans all clear, and his PET scan *cold*—Steve, AKA the Miracle Man, was declared CANCER FREE—a win by decision!

The doctors were pleased, but completely shocked. They knew their treatments were promising, but not one of them expected this. Each looked forward to Steve's check-up visits and spent more time with him than scheduled because his joy and zest for life were contagious. Duke even asked us to informally counsel and render moral support to other brain tumor patients and their families, which we happily did. People began to say they wanted to be more like Steve. Students, teachers, administrators, and parents alike even came to my classroom to ask for prayer as if I, too, had somehow become a sort of intercessor by proxy. Others just wanted to be near Steve; thus he developed a little following of young people who would visit him at the firehouse just hoping some of his—whatever you call it—would rub off on them as well.

By this time, Death must have been pacing the ring. How on Earth could this Miracle Man be doing so well? And cancer free? Could there have been some mistake? Big D must have kept checking his pickup card as doctors checked Steve's scans. He would look over their shoulders expectantly only to hear that he was a no-go. Death had pulled the card, by golly, and the cards had never really been wrong, had they?

Steve's brain was different after the surgery, though, and things were not perfect. We simply dubbed it NEW NORMAL. Sometimes Steve would mix up words or get tired, and I found that he could no longer tolerate the news or the action movies he once loved. He favored British comedies, *M*A*S*H*, and *How It's Made* as well as anything educational or uplifting—especially the beautiful documentary series *Planet Earth*. One day, I truly believed him healed when he came out in a self-fashioned costume as the bird of paradise from *Planet Earth*, executing the complete mating dance down to the last swoop. We laughed till it hurt that day, and I mistakenly assumed that we really pissed Big D off, because he made sure it never happened again. What never occurred to me was that perhaps Death had enjoyed the ridiculous dance as much as we had.

I did imagine that Death had watched this endless stream of positivity—reaching out to older neighbors, helping younger kids, praying for others, encouraging other brain tumor families, hosting wounded and depressed vets who left inspired—basically a parade of LIVING, and I figured that he had had enough. Like the Grinch at Christmas, all this living, living, living was excruciating! Perhaps his patience was wearing thin. There may have been fatigue in the Miracle Man's body, but that guy just wouldn't go down for the count, so I figured The Reaper decided to step into the ring, nothing personal, but he needed to end the round.

Chapter Four

Death Plays Rope-a-Dope

In boxing, it is generally assumed that the opponents will fight fair. No low blows, no sucker punches, and no cheap shots; however, there is a thing called strategy, and I naturally assumed Death was its master. While Steve was dancing around life's ring, ducking cancer's punches, bobbing and weaving away from its jabs, he was expending energy. When the opponent, disguised as cancer, dropped his guard, Steve began to pummel, thinking nothing of his own exhaustion, simply taking advantage of the opportunity to strike. Plainly speaking, while the cancer was in remission, Steve lived.

Someone asked him—and folks, YES, people will say some of the most absurd, asinine things to others during times such as these—how Steve was handling terminal cancer, "You know, how do you feel about dying from cancer?" His response to the "dying" statements was always to clarify, "You mean, how does it feel to live with cancer?" He was so used to talking and thinking like this that he believed it…or as Big D might reframe it—Steve fell for it.

I believed Death was so shocked at the worthiness of this Miracle Man that he had initially decided to allow him to prevail in the ring of life a bit longer. But the match was wearing on, too many rounds had passed, and Death was growing restless. So, he pulled the old Rope-a-Dope. Not really a slimy or sleazy trick, but a trick nonetheless where one boxer allows his opponent to pummel him, taking a few blows here and there just to wear the opponent out. The opponent grows ever bolder, thinking he has the upper hand, and will often fight even harder to finish up the match. That's when the contender ceases to be a punching bag and uses all that saved-up energy to turn it against the man who was heretofore winning. With all his might, Big D unleashed his pent-up energy—landing a hit here, a blow there, then without warning, Roping the Dope. Beating Miracle Man to a pulp because he could—at least that's how I saw it at the time.

Steve, so full of life, prancing around the ring, fancy footwork and fists flying, was spent and therefore no match for the Comeback Kid, the Deathanator, old Cancer Pants himself. Even the cheers of the crowd weren't enough to hold the opponent off; he came on anyway. Alas, the sounds of coaching and support of the team faded as Cancer Pants made mincemeat of the Miracle Man.

Again, it was summer, but it was 2009—a full two years after the Reaper expected to collect on his card. A year longer than the good doctor had given Steve *if* he received treatment, and I had noticed a change. I guess I had become the coach by now, knowing every sign, step, move, and glance of my champ…knowing every play in our book; therefore, when something tiny was amiss, I did not miss it this time.

The weather was ungodly hot, yet Steve told me he was cold. I assumed the air-conditioning was set too low as I was always too hot, so I adjusted it. Still he complained. Then he mixed up a few words—I panicked and phoned the neurologist, who assured me that all was well and that such a thing was normal after all Steve had been through. All empirical signs indicated that he was cured. He believed he was cured and I wanted to as well, but there was something...some tiny thing that kept poking the recesses of my mind and wouldn't stop.

School began, and things were falling into their routines with our work, but I noticed Steve sleeping a lot when I would arrive home when, in the past, he'd have been in his wood shop or weeding something. His doctors said naps were good and the scans had been clear, so I let it go, but that little voice...I now know what it was. It was our Uninvited Caller clinking his teacup in the corner of our living room, tapping his pencil, cracking his knuckles, doing all sorts of annoying little things to get my attention and let me know he was back...or that he had never truly left.

I could go on telling you our story in the past tense...but then you would only see Death as a villain. I've allowed him to be a bit of a bully, a creeper, sneaky and conniving thus far because those of us who've encountered him have felt pain. It's okay to see him as these things because anger at him is understandable and perhaps justifiable on all levels; however, I want you to also see him from a new perspective, and the only way to do that is to transport you right back into the moment—during our face-to-face.

So here, dear friends, is my **Caring Bridge Journal,** begun in response to the inundation of requests from well-meaning friends and family who called around the clock for daily updates on their beloved Steve. I wanted to give each person the good, the bad, or the ugly news myself, but there just wasn't enough of me to go around...not enough hours in the day. Therefore, when a friend suggested I start an online diary of sorts to report on Steve's progress with the return of his illness, it made sense. At the time it seemed logical, efficient, and useful—I had no idea it was going to be LIFE-changing...or rather, DEATH-changing.

Before I set up my **Caring Bridge.org** site, I read some samples of others', often moved to tears for them and their struggles, but one thing bothered me—the graphic detail some caregivers shared about their loved ones' conditions, complete with bodily functions, bowel habits, altered mental status, and information that was far too intimate and that denigrated the dignity of the patient. Many writers also chose to fixate on the looming specter of Death. Why, the Grim Reaper got so much press and was endowed with so much power that I vowed our site would be different. We would keep it positive just as Steve had intended, keep his message on track, but not sugarcoat the truth of what was happening to us. What purpose would that serve? No, we were going to keep to our plan of living, knowing that Big D had settled in on our couch, but we were going to attempt to make it very hard for him to call in his debt—hoping somehow to charm him away; and in so doing, we would grant him the same respect we would give Steve in the hope that we could all make peace and heal along the way.

This journal, along with Steve's unflagging optimism and our collective hope and joy, must have worked their magic on others, because what started merely to update friends and family on Steve's progress expanded to include thousands of worldwide readers, many of whom would urge me constantly to publish it as a book. I just couldn't do it. The thought, at the time, seemed seedy and almost cheap.

After…I couldn't even bear to look at it anyway, so I put it to rest in my mind. Years later, one friend was still so insistent I publish it that I finally said to her, "Laurie, I couldn't do that even if I wanted to—I have been locked out of my **Caring Bridge** site for the past five years because my old email no longer exists, and that email was the only administration address allowed to access my journal. I can't do this from memory, so I am afraid it is just too late now."

Two days later, and much to my utter surprise, my entire Caring Bridge Journal arrived in my new email inbox with a message from Laurie stating she knew I had to share it someday, that she had believed in it so much, she had saved it on her hard drive for the past seven years. Who does that? Wow! That was humbling to say the least.

In that case, I thought, perhaps it is worth sharing, and I now firmly believe Big D, or Morty, as his mother calls him, is in full agreement. So here it is—I invite you to re-experience it with me, or experience it for the first time yourself, but I bet you'll never look at Death the same way again.

Part Two

The Original Caring
Bridge Journal for
Steve Calloway

October 13, 2009

Hi everyone,

Hoping you all are well. We're trying to settle life down after getting Chelsea married, Mom moved to new Alzheimer's unit, and getting over the flu. Pray that Steve's headaches are just a mere remnant of his flu shot. Thanks for your interest and concern.

Love you all.

Hi all,

We're having Steve's thyroid checked to see if that's why his body temp is chronically low. His average temp ranges b/w 94 and 97... making him miserable most of the time—tired, achy. It doesn't help that I am struggling with hot flashes and need the house to be cool—he wins of course... Perhaps I'll have to get Steve a SNUGGIE! *

If it does turn out to be a thyroid problem (probably fried from previous radiation), then it's easily fixed. If not, we'll have to keep testing. Pray for an easy fix...we've been through enough tough fixes.

Love to you all

* Note: A SNUGGIE was a giant, adult-sized zip-up fleece sack with sleeves that was advertised on TV to ward off the cold. The commercials were overacted, showing shivering adults throwing temper tantrums with inadequate throw blankets until they ordered their SNUGGIES—a product that resembled sleeping bag meets footie pajamas. I suggest you YouTube it for a chuckle.

Hi All,

Just got the thyroid results, and Steve's thyroid is completely normal. The doc seemed happy, but it made me wonder at his symptoms. Was told that there are delayed reactions to radiation that can behave like this, but I guess we'll only truly know what's going on in Dec. with our next MRI. In the meantime, they've told us that Steve is perhaps trying to do too much…the only problem with that is that he won't say no to people who ask for help and favors. Sigh…what can ya do?

Keep us in your prayers, please, as we have you always in ours.

October 28, 2009

Hi folks,

Well, we're moving on to new testing to determine why Steve's body temp ranges between 94 and 97. If we can find that fix, he will not be walking around with perpetual hypothermia. I will hopefully be talking to the endocrinologist today about the latest ravages of radiation on the pituitary. Sigh. Please pray that the fix is as simple as another supplemental hormone, because Steve refuses to use a SNUGGIE—even though they now come in "attractive designer colors" such as cheetah and zebra!

God bless you all, and a special thank you to our new friend Farnaz from Tehran, who is praying for us daily at 4 a.m. and four more times a day...we are humbled by such faith and plan to keep that family in our prayers and hearts.

All love, jan

A light at the end of a long tunnel?

Got a call from our endocrinologist last night, and Steve is scheduled for in-hospital testing on Monday. Doc believes that thyroid test was a false negative, and he feels that the adrenals are involved as well. Should this prove true, he says we can fix it! Please thank God in your prayers for this hope, as it may help Steve feel human again. Thank you for your kind concern and prayers. We'll keep you posted.

love, jan

Hi All,

So now we wait... Spent most of yesterday at PRMC doing various blood tests, adrenal stimulation, thyroid screenings, etc. Steve had so much blood drawn and so many injections of various markers that he wobbled like a drunk to the car. He spent the rest of the day napping. We should know something by Thursday, and I was so pleased that Steve took the next three shifts off. He awoke quite dizzy and headachy today, so we want him quiet until we know the outcome of tests and (hopefully) begin new treatment.

Thank you all for asking after him and praying for him. He and I appreciate it so very, very much. I think the hardest part of this is that Steve is a "do-er," and he is wonderful at helping and taking care of others...it hurts him to have to be on the receiving end of things. He gets such joy out of working that rest, to him, is almost a punishment. We want him back on his feet with his hands in everything soon!

God bless you all, and I'll update you as soon as I know anything.
all love, jan

Hello All,

Well, we are back to square one. Endocrinologist said all tests were negative. Admittedly, I was upset initially, but he was pleased as it is quite difficult to balance multiple hormone levels artificially. We discussed that Steve's low temperature is responsible for the physical/mental discomforts—a function (or lack thereof) of the hypothalamus. This falls back under the purview of the neurologist, so we'll address it at our next MRI and appointment.

I was worried that Steve would be upset not to have a clear reason for the changes, but he was happy. He said, "Well, I must be fine then, and I'll just have to wear more layers and kick my own butt into action!" We will be investing in Under Amour thermal gear and high-calorie shakes to feed his furnace. One thing the doc DID say was that low body temps could lead to fatigue and foggy thinking, so we decided NOT to assume it's another tumor until we get the MRI results.

Once again…I am humbled by the resilience and positive attitude of my husband. I should copy him more and fret over him less. Keep us in your prayers…and invest in SNUGGIES!

all love, jan

November 9, 2009

Hi Everyone,

Welcome to those of you who are new to our site...we're glad you are here. To our "old friends," we are grateful for your continued concern, care, and prayers. Well, we've gotten Steve into Under Amour Cold Weather gear, and he's feeling warmer. He says it's a bit tight (I got the clingy version—woohoo), but he thinks it will serve him well. Hey, he'd wear anything to avoid the SNUGGIE!!!!

Headaches seem to have stabilized...not disappeared but are manageable with Advil. We'll of course know more when we see the neuro-oncologist next month. We prayed a lot about it and decided not to panic without good cause...a lot easier said than done. We literally had to visualize putting our fears in God's lap and walking away from them.

We thank you for your continued prayers, and we offer ours up for you. God bless you all, and remember to love each other,

jan

Hi everyone!

So glad you stopped in. If this thing would give you coffee, I'd pour you a cup and ask you to pull up a chair. Well, I guess you can do that where you are… Anyway…Steve went back to work today (after three shifts off) and left the house like a nervous schoolboy. It didn't take long, though, before he'd gotten his first call and was back to business as usual. While I don't

think any one thing helped him feel better, his decision to forge ahead seemed to renew some strength. I lost my voice today… throat sore…cough getting worse…and I started feeling sorry for myself.

Then I remembered Steve's cheery voice on the phone, and I managed to finish my school day. Besides…my students considered my laryngitis a complete blessing… Come to think of it… Steve did too!

Take care. Smile. Laugh. Hug. And eat plenty of fiber!
hugs, jan

Hello friends, family, and friends we've yet to meet!

I want to let you know that while we're counting our blessings, we will include each of you. You may not think I'm talking about YOU, but your kind little greetings, smiles in the hallways, pep talks on the cancer site, and funny emails that test my bladder strength are HUGE blessings in our lives. I believe God has used EACH of you to be His angels "with skin on." Thank you for responding to His nudges.

I just must tell you that I learned a valuable lesson just now from a lovely woman named Jenn who takes gratitude to new heights! Her hubby struggles with the same type of tumor as Steve's, yet she found the strength to encourage all of us with her extensive (and inclusive) gratitude list. Another amazing lesson comes from my pal Holly (whom I've never met in person) who takes time out of her busy days of caring for kids and for her hubby (with brain cancer) to check in on me and the other wives with words of love and laughter.

But the most poignant lesson has come from my beloved friend Sheila, who lost her soulmate Glenn this past September when he succumbed to his brain tumor. During her trial and struggle, mourning her love while nurturing her three young children, she has oozed grace, faith, peace, and loving gentleness. She is the kind of person I can only strive to be.

So, as we gobble our turkey and splay on the living room floor drunk with tryptophan…let's remember that we might not be a big deal in the world's eyes…but we might mean all the world to someone in our lives.

Thank you for always being there for us. Steve and I are so very grateful and will need a lifetime to pay all your kindnesses forward. Thank God for you.

all love, jan and Steve

A Thought from Sheila:

Safety in Numbers

In 2008 I was making one of our many visits to the Brain Tumor Center at Duke with my dear husband Glenn. Glenn was diagnosed with Glioblastoma Multiforme in January of 2007. We were told at Duke there was hope. At home, in New Jersey, we were told to prepare for the worst. I know that hearing there was hope is enough for many to carry on. For me it was nice, but I needed to really understand the truth about this disease. The truth is not an easy pill to swallow. I pressured the social workers, whose job it was to keep us positive, to be honest with me. On the trip prior to this one, as hard as it was for her, she was honest.

"Is it possible that my husband will not die from this disease?" I asked.

The answer was "no." That was the battle I had to deal with. I did not tell my husband. I could not tell him. He was not asking. He liked the idea of hope. I did not want to take this away from him. Everyone has their own way. Who was I to make him travel my journey? But I didn't know how to grapple with this. It was so hard to know he was going to leave us. Our children were quite young in 2008. We had three; one was just four years old, the other two were eight and eleven. I did not know how to handle my reality and not have him to talk to about it.

That day at Duke, I asked the social worker to pair me up with someone who was on this path with us. I had an incredible amount of support from family and friends, but I just felt that having someone in the same position would be helpful. I knew there had to be some-one else who could need me as well. On that day, I was given Jan's phone number. On that trip, Jan and Steve were in the same hotel getting ready for appointment follow-ups just as we were. We met for coffee. From that moment and the many going forward, I was no longer alone.

Jan and I really seemed to understand each other. We didn't want to be on this journey, but we were not going to be alone any longer. We were going to support each other the best we could. As widows, we still do the same. If I have learned anything from this part of my life, I learned that you should always ask for help whenever you need it, and there is always a force that you can tap into that will guide you if you are open to it. It is not magic, but it feels damn close.

Shelia Grifo Fredericks, Widow's Walk Support Group

Hi everyone.

It hurts to have to write this, but Steve is in our regional ICU. He appeared to have stroke-like symptoms yesterday, but further testing revealed a new tumor—a fast grower as the August scans were clear. They have not determined whether it is a recurrent tumor or new primary one unrelated to the first. Our neurosurgeon is sending scans to Duke to see if it is operable or not and to determine the best treatment options. At present, Steve is unable to talk, walk, or swallow, and he is sleeping most of the time. They say this is good as he is completely exhausted. Pray for a timely response from our Duke team.

It has been said, "The wound is the place where the Light enters you." — Rumi.

That must make us LIGHT BEINGS.

I ask for your continued prayers and for all of us to keep our faith in the healing grace of God.

All shall be well…no matter what.

Love you all, so take care of each other. Jan

Dear friends and prayer partners,

I am once again overwhelmed, touched, and humbled by your outpouring of love, kind words, and prayers. They are so very important now, and please believe me that each of you is in my daily prayers. I am so very lucky to have you all in my life. The latest news is that Duke is in the loop and awaiting our latest scans to help them decide between surgery and chemo. Steve's vital signs are stable, and he is sleeping most of the time. The staff believes that he's been struggling with this tumor for weeks now which has left him exhausted, so sleep is a good thing. I must share this next bit with you though, because you all know what kind of a guy Steve is. I was called back for a consult with the speech pathologist who was assessing Steve's speech and ability to swallow. As I walked the long, long hall of the new ICU, I saw our nurse peek out of the room and whisper, "She's coming!" As I rounded the doorway, the pathologist was tapping out a beat on Steve's leg as she exclaimed, "Come on, Steve, just like we practiced, one, two, three," and he turned to me, cheek sagging, lips twisted, eyes squeezed tightly in concentration and managed a strained but determined "I – WUB – YOU!"

It was glorious…perfect…the best Christmas present I could ever hope to receive! To anyone else, it might have sounded like gibberish…but to me it was sheer poetry. No dry eyes anywhere in that room. You see—tumors may take your voice, your strength, and your balance…but they can never touch your spirit. Steve's spirit and loving soul are completely intact, and I am the luckiest woman in the world.

I promise to keep you posted, but for now I cherish your prayers. God is at work here, as always, and His little miracles take place all around…be sure to look for them.

I love you all, jan

December 2, 2009

Hi everyone,

Today was better for all of us. The steroid (dexamethasone—Decadron) is working to reduce the swelling around Steve's tumor, and I'm happy to report that some of his important functions are improving. He was able to swallow today, with weakness only in his mouth, not esophagus. This meant that he could eat mashed potatoes, peaches, and pudding—any child's menu of choice! The speech therapist was shocked when Steve could say partial phrases, but Steve would then get frustrated that he could not finish a single thought...something that brought him to tears. His facial droop is now less pronounced, and he can even smile a bit on his right side. I KNEW he was improving when he winked at me with each of his eyes in turn. Hubba hubba!

The physical therapists got him to stand up, toddle a step or two, and sit in a chair. They then handed him his gourmet lunch. Ever eager to show us all that he was a fighter, he took the spoon from the therapist and proceeded to proudly feed himself. He was grinning his little lopsided grin with pudding on his cheek and chin, and I was as proud as any new mother of her newly "independent" toddler!

He quickly tired, however, as the day progressed, and any attempts at sharing his fears and discussing his condition ended in sobs. How painful it must be to want to talk out one's disappointment, one's fear, and one's plan for healing...yet have no way to express any of it. Even so, each time after tears rolled down his cheek, he would gather himself, sigh, smile, and say, "I love you."

Somehow, "I love you" fixes everything…and in the end…it's all that matters. I've just been informed that he'll be moving to a step-down unit—forward progress—until we hear the game plan from Duke.

Thank you for your prayers, and remember…when fancy words fail you, when clever thoughts leave you, and when tears threaten to flow…there's always "I love you."

And we do.

December 3, 2009

Hi Gang...what a difference a day can make. Days—and lives—can turn on a dime. I guess the answer is to find a calm center so that you don't notice the crazy spinning so much. Here's the rundown: At 3 a.m., while in his new quieter step-down room, Steve began having seizures that have lasted all day—sometimes as minor as a facial twitch and sometimes with full-on paralysis... but never ceasing.

Meds were added, increased, and tweaked, but as of this minute (11:45 p.m.) the twitch remains. As a result, he's been taken back off food. The nurse and I decided tonight that we would try bathing him to settle him down, and I shaved his head and face. That helped to soothe his exhausted body, and he's in a deeper sleep now than he's been all day. But I am also sure the deep loving concern of his nurses and neurosurgeon has contributed greatly to his peace.

It never ceases to amaze me that Steve has such a power to move people to be their best selves. With stumbling, often incoherent words, he captures hearts and inspires souls. With his trembling thank-yous and crooked smiles, he brought the staff together to pray over him...nurse, tech, orderly, custodian, and neurosurgeon. Standing around him, holding hands, the differences melted away, titles were shucked to the floor, and minds united in prayerful requests for healing of this good, sweet man.

As day progressed, the wait for Duke to respond to Steve's new tumor with a treatment plan began to make everyone on the PRMC team nervous. I found myself start to join them when I remembered something a friend once told me. "God answers in His own time...but always IN time." I repeated that as a mantra several times until my phone suddenly rang...after working hours...with a call from our neuro-oncologist at Duke. YAY!

We shared our sorrow over the new tumor, vowed to hug each other properly in person, and discussed our options. We determined together that Steve is not a candidate for another surgery, but he IS for a new drug trial that has met with success. Our job here is to limit seizure activity and encourage rest, and Dr. D's job is to set up our visit to Duke this week.

So now, as the clock marks the end of this day, I realize that what threatened to destroy our peace and faith, what tried to derail our healing and send us spinning out of control, was eclipsed by something much more powerful—the unflagging, unshakeable, indefatigable love and trust in God's care. And, His lifeline in the form of a treatment plan arrived...right on time.

All love, jan

December 5, 2009

Hey Everyone,

I slacked off on updating last night mainly because we brought Steve home—a long and arduous process. Anyone who's stayed in the hospital knows that first they tell you you're going home, then the patient gets excited and rushes to get dressed, and then they subject you to five-plus hours of "one more thing before we release you. By the time the wheelchair shows up, you've forgotten where home actually is.

Luckily for me my brother Kent was on hand to help with the transition, to remind us where we live, pick up all the new meds, go to the grocery store, help move Steve into the house, and pick up the walker. He was so busy and productive I thought he was a woman!! Oh, just kidding, men...

Steve did well to navigate around the house, and his first act was to make a pot of coffee...but he was highly offended that I had to add thickener to his brew to prevent him from aspirating it. I got what we rednecks call the "stink eye," and he ignored me for half an hour. Some things are sacred, and apparently coffee is one of them.

Our son Mac made it in from New York as well, and we all relaxed together before the first round of meds was due. Steve tolerated them well, but they don't work as fast as IV drugs, so we had to deal with some seizure activity. As Steve's job #1 is to rest, we are limiting visitors—but we know well how many of you love him, are praying for him, and are rooting for his return to health! We'll send word when he's ready for guests.

Duke should inform us on Monday as to our treatment start-date, and speech, occupational, and physical therapy should resume then as well. Until then, I must assume all three, and I've been told by brother, son, and Steve that I'm bossy. I am highly indignant...just because I hover, instruct, scold, and direct? I'm sure if you asked ANY of my students, they would be completely confused over that. (hee hee hee)

Well, it's time for the next round of treatment, so I will sign off for now. However, let me just tell you what has helped me get through thus far, and what will surely help in the days to come: No matter what is happening, whether good or horrid, I try my hardest to repeat, "All is well, all is well, and all shall BE well." If you do it enough...it begins to sink in. After all, what I can do—I do...and what I can't—God does. So, where's the need or room for worry?

Thank you for NOT worrying with me and lifting Steve in prayer instead. Now excuse me while I must go give orders.

All love, jan

December 8, 2009

Hi there everybody,

Well, for those of you who tell me how strong and uplifting I am, I'm going to burst that imaginary and unwarranted bubble. You see, we've re-entered the realm I had conveniently repressed since Steve's first tumor…a realm I haven't had the pleasure to enter since the days of newborn babies. <cue ominous music> I call this realm: DECADRON NIGHTS…and it ain't pretty.

For those of you who are new to the miracle drug we caregivers love to hate, Decadron is a strong steroid necessary to keep brain swelling under control for the viability of the patient; but something so powerful and effective brings along a host of side effects from lowered immunity to sleepless nights. It's a sneaky little devil, just doing its thing beautifully until it's fostered a sense of well-being; then it turns all Jekyll and Hyde and begins waking the patient at 3 a.m.—and I mean WIDE awake.

During the first tumor, Steve would get up, move to the couch, and watch TV…and I would try to fall back to sleep. However, this time, Steve must be accompanied and monitored always, so 3 a.m. is now wake-up time for us both, and if I try to get him to stay in bed "a few more minutes" he gets frustrated and doesn't understand…kind of like a newborn. So, now nights consist of getting in bed, sleeping a couple of hours, waking him up at midnight for his meds, dropping back off, then up for good at 3 a.m.

Thankfully he naps during the day—crucial for healing his brain—but that's the only time I can get chores done, so I miss out on the day sleep. Compared to his situation, my lack of sleep isn't a crisis…but it does wear one down so that when well-wishers call for updates or show up at the door, my smile isn't as quick as it should be, and if I don't seem as with it or responsive, you'll know it isn't you. It's just that I am back in the era of tending to a newborn…except that I'm older now and I don't have that new mommy glow.

Now, to look on the bright side…and there's ALWAYS a bright side, Steve is improving overall. He can now eat without choking and drink his beloved coffee. He's getting better with the walker and maneuvers it well. He shaved and dressed himself—a milestone skill required to be approved for the drug trial, and he even remembered how to say my name!!!

His mind is still keen, it's just trapped in a body that struggles to form coherent words, but I'm getting better at deciphering them—so all that Latin I teach is coming in handy. He managed to tell me how tiring it is to know what's going on but be unable to express his thoughts and feelings fluently. We've tried writing, but that expression meets with the same blocks. He's getting better each day though, so your prayers are surely working. And I really mean that.

Another little anecdote: When words DO come for Steve, sometimes they closely resemble the word he's fishing for—enough so that I get it, and sometimes it's so endearing I want to cry. Last night, he dropped his head before dinner, and I asked if he was okay. He said, "Sure, I was just talking to Bob." Lack of sleep slowed my comprehension and I asked, "Bob?" Steve nodded vigorously and pointed upward. "Yes, BOB! He make me better!" Suddenly my dim little lightbulb went on and I realized that I needed to thank Bob—aka God—too.

And, I thank BOB for all of you…your sweet, sweet emails, your calls, your cards, your offers of food, and most important of all, your prayers. I know that BOB will bless you for your kindnesses as he's already blessed us with you.

All love, jan

December 9, 2009

Hi gang!

What started to be a tempestuous and nasty day has turned into a delightful afternoon. Wind and pelting rain this morning, now warm sunshine, complete with good reports from the nurses and a start date from Duke for treatment. We were even able to venture out on the sidewalk for a breath of fresh air. Here's what happened...

Moving at a snail's pace behind Steve and his walker, I told myself to slow down and relax—I had nowhere else to be. It was a good thing too, or in my haste and impatience I might have missed another one of God's amazing little miracles.

That's something I've noticed during this whole incredible whirlwind of medical drama—we all seem fixated on the BIG MIRACLE...the healing of a brain tumor. Soon, our fervent prayers become singular in focus, targeted, and almost fierce. Don't get me wrong...they're necessary and good, but we forget that God works on all levels, many of which we miss when we're on our knees white-knuckling our way through desperate pleas. I'm beginning to see that these answers to prayer rarely come in lightning bolts, thunder claps, or parting of the waters, but rather in quiet, little unfoldings that require a simple, still mind and heart.

If I weren't padding along softly behind Steve in my furry slippers, I might have missed this one, but even if I were too distracted, few of God's blessings get past Steve. "Look at that!" he exclaimed, grinning and pointing to one of our gray, withered rosebushes. "It's US!" Any other time I might have missed the two perfect little roses, clinging bravely to a shriveled twig, dancing in the wind. All around them things were dying, waterlogged, and colorless, but they didn't seem to notice. Their little faces were turned to the sun, petals unfurled awaiting a cosmic hug.

Two roses blooming in December…who would've thought it possible? I was so shocked I took pictures, but Steve seemed to take it in stride, albeit with great joy. You see, what seems to be an anomaly or miracle to me seems perfectly delightful, yet not surprising, to Steve. It's almost as if he just KNOWS God has sent him another little love note as a sign of His undying affection.

"Yep," I answered, "they ARE us! Shall we pick them?"

Steve paused, thought, and replied, "No, they happy in sun." Then he tapped his heart and added, "Besides, they in here."

And he was right…again. There was no need to cut and capture the little floral love notes…because God sends them all the time if we just open our eyes…and hearts…and know Him on a first-name basis—Bob.

FACE-TO-FACE with BOB

Hello Dear Friends and Fam,

If you're reading this on Sunday, then you can pray proactively, thanking God for our first treatment noon tomorrow at Duke, and if you're reading this on Monday, pray, thanking God that our day is going smoothly, and the treatment is doing its job. Also, if you're feeling spiritual, say a prayer of thanks that our insurance company will cover these procedures...because as of now they're undecided.

On to happier subjects...Steve and I were talking last night, and he expressed concern that our friends/family would be discouraged by the recurrence of the tumor and would therefore blame or doubt God. Steve knows his first tumor healing was a miracle, and honestly his latest improvement defies the doctors' predictions; but Steve is adamant that God is not a one-trick pony, and we recalled (both at once) Steve's encounter with his "angel." Suddenly, things really came into focus.

In spring of 2008, as Steve was at the oncologist's office awaiting his infusion of chemo, he perched on the edge of the exam table, wondering if his blood work would be okay so that drugs could be administered. After a few minutes, the door opened, and an older, somewhat weathered man entered and closed the door behind him. He was smiling and confident, so Steve assumed he was a partner in the practice who just happened to be in casual clothing. The man removed his ball cap and shook Steve's hand vigorously.

"Good morning! How are we today?" the man asked with a warm smile and sat on the doctor's stool. Steve assured him that God had healed him and that he was better each day (Steve never answers otherwise). "Well, that's good," answered the man, "you are healed, but I want you to remember something…these things might return, but you'll just deal with each situation as it arises and get your treatments, and everything will be okay. Just don't get discouraged; there are a lot of things at work here."

Then the man stood up, patted Steve on the arm, said good-bye smiling, and stepped out. Steve was happy to have met him but wondered if the man was another doctor or perhaps another patient just being friendly and supportive. A minute later, the nurse opened the door to drop off Steve's chart, so he asked her whether the man was a doctor or patient.

"What man, Steve?"

"The older man who just walked out. Didn't you see him?"

"Steve, are you hallucinating? I've been sitting outside this door at my desk, and I'm telling you there hasn't been anyone in or out."

Just then it dawned on Steve that this wasn't any doctor's call or casual meeting with another albeit friendly patient…this was a face-to-face with someone much more influential.

"So, Steve, at the time you told me you believe you'd met an angel… Do you still believe that?" I asked him.

"I wonder now…maybe it was an angel…or maybe I came face-to-face with BOB. All I know is that I liked him a whole, whole lot."

So, as you go throughout your days, remember to think before you jump to judgment...that craggy old man, that young dirty-faced child, that annoying, pushy person in line might be here to tell you something important. Be nice, no matter what, for you may be entertaining angels unaware...or perhaps even Bob Himself.

Dear Loved Ones—the ones we know and have yet to know,

How do we even begin to express adequate gratitude for such an amazing outpouring of loving support? I think a simple "thank you" just doesn't cut it.

Each time I write these updates, I try to wait for Bob (God) to give me some guidance, inspiration, whatever… and it just flows. This time, I feel the message so intensely that I can barely type fast enough to keep up. I will try to do my best to get it right and get ME out of the way. —jan

Here's Bob:

My dear children…I'm glad you enjoyed hearing about Steve's angel and the wonderful things I'm doing in his life. I know that you struggle to understand the suffering I'm allowing, but you of course cannot see the big picture as I do. Often children do not understand constrictions placed by a loving parent, but trust that I have Steve's best interest at heart and that all will be blessed tenfold by this experience.

Did you know that I surround you with angels all the time? Most of the time you never realize it, and I find it curious that so many of you think that you don't deserve them or my blessings, but you are my beloved children and I bless you no matter what you do. Sometimes, you lower your guard long enough to see these beings or feel them, and I notice that when you begin to look for them, you are delighted and amazed by their presence.

What you may not realize at all is that I do have other angels…not the ethereal, flying kind…but rather the down-to-earth (no pun intended…well, okay, intended) skin-on kind. And, my children, these angels are YOU.

You see, my precious ones, you get to be angels for each other. You don't have to be rich, pretty, popular, smart, or ambitious. You don't have to be religious, holy, or pious. You just must do one small thing.

Oh, you want to know what that ONE SMALL THING is… Well, I can't tell you because you already know. It is nestled in your heart, ready to flow out. And when it does, you begin a current which suddenly flows out, creating a vacuum that draws in love, light, and liquid joy that floods your being. You know what I'm talking about…that delicious feeling when you love each other and surprise each other with simple little kindnesses. It is one of my greatest gifts and one of the easiest to experience!!

It only requires a gesture, a thought, a smile, a hug, a word, a prayer, but its impact is exponential. Then, I take that one small thing, and oh, if you could just see what I do, you would see how I magnify it to spread goodness and love…the things miracles are made of!!!

Some of you marvel at the blessings that seem to flow to Steve and Jan, but I find it funny that you are surprised. Don't you realize that YOU are the miracle? YOU are the angels? YOU are the healing?

You are the one who took a picture of a little boy's smile and sent it; you are the one who sends pictures of your smiling baby;

you are the one who mailed that beautiful card; you are the one who responded to the emails letting Steve and Jan know you are there and listening; you are the one who baked cookies for their trip to Duke; you are the one who encouraged high schoolers to write messages of hope, or middle schoolers to make ornaments, or lower schoolers to pray and create a book of healing. You are the one who made soup and loaned Steve a blessed medal. You are the one who drove Jan to and from the hospital, fetched groceries, and brought up dinner. You are the one who sent the Caring Bridge site to your family in NC who then offered up their home near Duke. You are the one who gets on your knees in Iran at 4 a.m. every morning to tell me about Steve. You are the one who puts his name on a prayer list. You are the one who reassured Steve and Jan of their future job security. You are the one who offered to mow the lawn for Steve. You are one who picks up their mail, takes out their trash, and lovingly puts the porch light on. You are the one who steps in for Jan, giving her classes excellent instruction. You are the ones who picked up her slack, taking duties, chaperoning trips, reassuring kids, and keeping the Random Acts of Kindness Club going.

And YOU are the ones who do the most important angel activity of all—you pray and tell ME how much you love Steve and Jan and how much you want their healing. I hear you...I hear you...I hear you.

You are my beloved children, and I love you no matter what, but you make my heart sing and my heavens rejoice when you are my little angels with skin on.

So, as you go through your day, remember that sometimes I allow bad things to happen, because in that suffering, there is manifested extraordinary beauty and grace that you would otherwise miss.

So, go on now and do that one small thing, and let ME worry about the big picture.

I love you, my children, Bob

December 18, 2009

Hi Everyone,

First, please pray for my friend Holly and her hubby, S—, as they go through the grueling wait for biopsy and MRI results. Holly would never dwell on the difficult as she's one of the most positive and loving people I know. Also, keep Charlie in your prayers as he's struggling on a new trial which nails the tumor, but kicks him in the gut too.

Thanks…you are all such wonderful prayer partners that I KNOW good things will result.

Now as for us. The good news is that Steve told me today, "Bob (God) has healed me again…He's got something in mind with this new treatment, so I'll just go along for the ride." I know he's right because Steve and Bob are tight.

The bad news is that Steve has been struggling on the new treatment that started on Monday at Duke. The first day after, he was tired, but sharper, clearer. Then came Wednesday and the crushing fatigue and weakness. He sleeps for hours in the day— his best method of healing—and is rejuvenated for a while, but if he is up for just a hair too long, his knees buckle, or he seizes mildly. And tonight, he slurred his words again.

In addition, he's immunocompromised, so any visitors must mask up, and we can't go out in public for fear of infection while his white count is so low. His EMS buddies are discouraged from visiting because of their exposure to germs, and their presence would be helpful right about now.

I know these are benchmarks of the treatment process, but they take us on such an emotional roller-coaster that we should just throw up our hands and scream...as long as we secure all loose items and keep hands and feet in the vehicle at all times! So...now I will ask for some specific prayers, and I will hope that I'm not being too selfish or greedy:

1. Obliteration of this tumor/ perfectly clean brain

2. Manageable symptoms during treatment

3. Maintaining a good white blood cell count

4. More than two to three hours of sleep each night (both of us)

5. Ability of Jan to return to work as we've no real income at present

6. Grace to ride the waves with peace, smiles, and humility

We send all love, and we hope your holidays are filled with joy and harmony.

Love each other...that's all that matters. jan

Hi Guys,

Today is Steve's and my fifth anniversary. Although we met later in
life…we love each other as if years
were behind us. Steve tried to write
me something, but his mind/hand/
language centers won't sync up; I
did manage to identify "Jan" and
"love" and "forever"…and that's
plenty good enough for me.

No matter what happens, however, our love WILL last forever.

In His Hands, jan

December 22, 2009

Greetings from the land of the one-inch blizzard!

Christmas is only three days away, and I think I'm ready… It's going to be a small affair this year, but a gift from some very wonderful people (you know who you are) has helped so very much—thank you. We'll have a full house on Thursday as daughter Chelsea and her husband Dave arrive from Texas. Son Mac arrived last Friday and has been a terrific help. He even told me to go take a long nap the other day—I guess the exhaustion was written all over my face—and he looked after Steve as well as any professional nurse. Isn't it interesting how these trials can bring us to our best selves? I don't think I've slept so well in weeks—thanks, Mac.

Steve is sleeping A LOT lately, and the tumor team at Duke is discussing his meds. We'll know tomorrow if we can scale back on a few to give Steve a little more energy. The neuro-oncology nurse said that while the chemo should leave him weak, Steve should not necessarily be this tired. Case-in-point: though Steve and I love his physical therapist, Steve breathed an exhausted sigh and collapsed on the couch at the end of their session. He was even too tired to retreat to the MAN CAVE—his workshop where he can sit, listen to Christmas carols, drink coffee, and drop cigar ash with reckless abandon on the floor.

For those of you loving, well-meaning purists who cringe or puff up with indignation at the thought of a cancer patient puffing on a stogie, think about it. When you can't drive, when you are forced to use a walker, must down handfuls of meds and have others injected repeatedly into your veins to shrink a fast-growing brain tumor, a cigar is the least of your worries. The Duke doc even said, "Leave him alone about the cigars." So, to our altruistic yogic, organic, kinesthetic, and sometimes pedantic friends—let it go, and understand that a momentary pleasure for a man with a brain tumor is not the battle to pick this time.

Now, beloved ones, lest you think me rude, please know that we cherish your attentions, and we covet your prayers. I can't tell you how much they mean to us—and receiving lovely messages that you are praying for him literally brings a grin to Steve's face. He said, "Bob (aka God) will be so sick of hearing about Steve Calloway that He'll heal me just to shut them all up so He can get some peace!"

So, when you pray, may I ask that you pray for a perfect pink brain and shining vitality for Steve, and also for our other GBM (tumor) friends: Steven, Gary, Charlie, Tim, Ed, Rob, Mary, Andy, Shari, Sondra, Craig M., Shahrokh (and others)—a dubious, yet ever growing club to which we wish we never belonged.

And, while you're on your knees...put in a word for world peace and the end to global hunger. Hey...what the heck, if your knees are as creaky as mine, you need to maximize the opportunity!

We love you all,
Jan n Steve

Wow...I recall recently saying (rather piously I might add) that things can turn on a dime. At the time I was referring to something positive, but alas (as with the Taoist wheel of life) things can turn 180 degrees in no time.

Early this morning, around 1:30, Steve awoke with projectile vomiting. I managed to get him to the bathroom, but there he collapsed, limp on his right side. Luckily, Mac had fallen asleep on the couch and heard my cry for help and lifted Steve to the bed. We called the ambulance and ended up in the ER of AGH—our local hospital. For the next seven hours, we got excellent and compassionate care by the ER team, and Steve has since been admitted.

He has a terrible stomach virus, which explains days of weakness and excessive sleeping, but we're not exactly sure why the reappearance of weakness on the right side, the aphasia (garbled speech), and difficulty swallowing—did his intracranial pressure rise during the nausea?

The Duke neuro-oncology nurse called, and everyone has agreed on another MRI. We'll keep you posted on the results. I will not speculate here as to what is behind the setback in function—it could resolve tonight, or it could be a new chapter for us in this saga. Either way, the BIG GUY in the SKY is gonna have to support me on this one. My bag of positive attitude is in sore need of replenishment.

So, I will ask for your prayers that this is merely a temporary setback on the road to recovery. I am smiling out of sheer determination at this stage…and I finally understand a quote I once heard about courage:

"Courage is not the ABSENCE of fear, rather the ACKNOWLEDGMENT of fear while forging ahead anyway." I guess I'll try to keep on keeping on.

Love you all…

Hello everyone!

There's a snap in the air and a jingle in my spirit. This is the day that the Lord has made, so let us rejoice!!!! And there is ALWAYS something to rejoice about... For example, I've met another angel named Priscilla, who has big beautiful brown eyes and mocha-colored skin. She brings sunlight into the room and oozes love with every linen change. She takes immense pride in keeping her patients comfortable, which in turn keeps their spirits up. She would never claim to do anything fancy, but she has been a HUGE part of our fantastic healing team at Atlantic General! Don't ever, ever underestimate the power of the job you do. You can change and enhance lives in every vocation, every day.

Well, today is the day that we're going to turn that penny "HEADS UP"! We're going to turn those frowns upside down (you want to pinch me, don't you?). Where some might say, "Steve has a significant weakness on his right side," we are seeing a hand squeeze and a wiggle of the foot. Where some see a significant speech deficit, we're hearing phrases and Steve's sense of humor. For instance, when breakfast arrived, a starving Steve opened the lid on the bowl to find chicken broth. He then cut his eyes up at me, smirked, and uttered his characteristically dry, "My..." And later when he finally convinced them to give him real food, he savored his hot turkey, grunting like a pig and rolling his eyes. When I asked him what he thought, he said, "Oh, this is SO bad, but chewy!"

Yes, Steve's sense of fun is re-emerging, and I've noticed Bob's (aka God) is too. I mean I seriously think I've been celestially punked! I can recall reading a friend's Caring Bridge site, marveling at the amount of hands-on care our friend required that his wife lovingly provided. I said a prayer for them and thanked God for my highly functioning survivor husband. I distinctly remember telling God that I wasn't one of those strong people who could handle that kind of physical need or challenge, and that I was happy that He'd not given me "more than I could handle." I think that's when Bob got the idea...

Bob heard me all right...and He knew that I was going to have to be brought into such things by the back door. You know, like a frog in a pot of boiling water??? If you drop it directly in, the frog leaps out in shock, but if you plop it in lukewarm water and SLOWLY turn up the heat, he doesn't notice and before long—he's cooked!

So, there I was, convincing the hospital team to let me take Steve home, not to a rehab center, because I knew that would kill him—emotionally—as he desperately wants to be home. I assured them that I had a big, strong son, son-in-law, and daughter waiting at home, and lots of burly and eager firemen just itching to lift something. In the middle of all this scheming, I changed Steve's linens with Priscilla, cleaned him up, and lifted him back in place as he can't maneuver by himself. Then, as I was balling up the soiled sheets and washing my hands, I caught a glimpse of myself in the mirror.

There I was...almost bald (I used to be so vain about my hair but cut it all off when Steve's fell out—I don't miss it one bit), no makeup (I must look lovely because nurses keep offering me oxygen), and in an oversized sweater and jeans (so comfy, but *What Not to Wear* could show up at any minute)…and then it hit me—I was doing that job that I told God I could never handle. I guess the difference is simply…love.

I know that the most important thing to the man I love is not what waits UNDER the Christmas tree; it is simply SEEING the tree from his own couch. So, I guess I've been simmerin' in the pot without realizing it. All I can say is JUMP IN! The water's great!!!!! (Thank you, Priscilla.)

all love, jan

Our dear friends,

Although we didn't get released on Christmas Eve, Dr. A stayed true to his promise to have Steve home for Christmas on the couch! We were home by 10 a.m., and had son Mac, son-in-law Dave, and daughter Chelsea awaiting the emancipated Steve. It was a good thing, because we've had a significant setback—I didn't want to say anything yesterday as I didn't want to mar your celebrations. It appears that what we initially thought was just a nasty virus was masking an ischemic stroke (blockage in blood flow within his brain).

This IS a two-sided penny though, because the MRI also showed necrotic tissue around the tumor, which means IT IS DYING and the MEDS ARE WORKING!!! The downside (that GBM-ers know all too well) is that Av— (one of the working chemo drugs) can cause strokes. So, while it is saving Steve's life, Av— is potentially eroding his function.

I was trying to figure out how to be happy about our progress while practical about the effects of a stroke, with thoughts of wheelchairs and ramps racing through my head. That was when the doc stated that Steve should make significant recovery as some of his faculties were already returning within forty-eight hours of the attack. From Monday night to Thursday, he was able to move his right foot, squeeze the doc's hand, swallow without difficulty, and control his bladder. We were all so excited and encouraged that we failed to see the whole picture.

"The Rubber Ball," as the docs labeled Steve—because he

always bounces back—didn't quite have as much function as we thought, and we weren't totally prepared for our homecoming. There was too much weakness for Steve to use the walker, and we should have had a wheelchair. We also realized shower seat and grab bars would be necessary as well, but because it was Christmas day, every supplier was closed. So, we walked Steve to and fro between us all day—resembling fraternity brothers escorting home a drunken buddy. It worked after we rearranged ALL the furniture to clear pathways, but only because there were four of us. As much as I hate to admit this, I could not do this on my own, and Steve's independence has been seriously compromised.

If I pray hard, I will be able to handle this somehow, but funds are stretched thin, my income on hold while I'm out on leave, and Steve's disability not equal to his former salary. If I go right back to work, I will have to hire full-time help (this is more than friends and neighbors can handle), which will break the bank, and if I stay home, we are financially slammed as well.

So, please bear with me as I dig out from under this weighty info. I wrestled with not sharing until I'd gotten in control of my attitude, but I knew I needed to let you know about his setback. Please keep us in your prayers—pray for fast recovery, steady income, and continued healing from the tumor...oh, and for joy and peace—they would be nice. Hope that's not too much to ask.

Love you all...stand by...I promise good news later...I have faith!

Cue Music from THE GOOD, THE BAD, AND THE UGLY

Today's entry is not for the faint of heart…a message from the DARK SIDE of brain cancer…

I wish I could be the voice of inspiration tonight. I wish I could give you a great story of amazing healing, but I think all I can offer at this moment is the TRUTH—the ugly, uncharitable, cold, raw truth. Here's something I've been thinking a lot about. And trust me, I have a lot of time to think. I am going on night #4 without sleep…but more on that in a minute. I will try to decompress for a few minutes before trying to lie down. I'm so tired I'm wigged out at this moment, so if you can handle it…read on.

So, I finally convinced Steve to sleep in the bed tonight as opposed to the couch. As I tucked him in, he said, "I'll be up soon and come back out." It broke my heart on two levels—realizing that he wants to stay connected, while also realizing that he'll be up another night again, and "getting up" is a whole production with wheelchair, lifting, dressing him again (he wants to be dressed), and returning to the family room to surf the channels until dawn with me right there of course.

The kids came home to help—which they did as long as they could hold out. Then Chelsea and her hubby ended up in ER with that plague of a virus (norovirus) that leveled Steve. Mac was taking care of them and cooking for us all while I managed to hold off vomiting with Steve's anti-nausea meds; but the full impact of the illness got me last night, and I spent it trying to keep my head from splitting open and my fever under control. I dragged an air mattress down, so I could be more comfortable on the floor next to Steve's couch—good idea in theory—but every time Steve would become alert, he would also become instantly annoyed, declaring, "All you are doing is lying there, sleeping..." (ironically funny in a way). I would look at the clock, see that it was 1 a.m., 2 a.m., 3 a.m. and tell him it's still nighttime.

He couldn't seem to comprehend what that meant and would then ask for a drink, bathroom break, food, cigar (not smoking anymore though), or to have channel changed, TV turned down, blanket fixed, TV off, etc., etc., etc... I felt horrible, but by morning, I was snapping at this poor, confused, sweet man.

Okay, so here's the part I've been pondering for days now: I've heard a lot of folks give me advice which on the surface sounds plausible. As a matter of fact, I have recently offered it with good intentions to my other brain tumor friends. Now I think I owe them an apology. One popular suggestion is "You need to get some rest when Steve sleeps." Well, since he only sleeps during the day, I must balance my "rest" with laundry, meds, meals, insurance nightmares, money worries, and trying to get answers about disability, home-care, etc. which can only be done during business hours. Then, if I do lie down on the floor next to the couch for a nap, the phone rings.

The second bit of advice is: "You need to get some help." Well, yes, I agree...but help needs to truly be of help—not just people coming to see what Steve looks like or to tell me about their problems, because neither Steve nor I have any energy to talk anymore; and I have literally worn my son Mac out with cooking, trips to store, lifting, etc…

The third bit of advice is: Go back to work ASAP, because "you need the change of scenery, or a break, or the money…" Again, it sounds good, but THINK about the issue here: I am exhausted getting no sleep at night. How will getting up and teaching 120 teens in the day, then coming home to resume full-time care of a wheelchair patient be a "good change"? Also, until the darned insurance company lets me know if they'll even begin to help, I must be sure that the home care aide doesn't cost more per day than I make.

The next bit of advice is: "Hang in there… God doesn't give you more than you can handle." You know, I have said that to many people over the years, and I have really believed it, and I still believe it today. But I will never say that to anyone EVER again. Somehow, there's absolutely NOTHING comforting about hearing it.

Now for the good news. Okay, you are wondering if there IS good stuff… Well, yes, there is. Over the years, I have read a ton of books on God, spirituality, Zen, self-awareness, and forgiveness, and I have tried to change my thinking, my heart, and my faith. I felt reasonably well connected with God, and I somehow convinced myself that I was developing some maturity. But the thing is, sometimes you just don't have a relationship with God, maturity, or even grace without this raw, gut-wrenching suffering.

I read about patience, wanted to have it, but never developed it. I read about selfless service, wanted to be good at it, but never achieved it. I read about relying on God, wanted to do it, but only talked a good game of it. I read about mercy, wanted to think I showed it, but never was tested on it. Finally, I read about grace, wanted to possess it, but never attained it. Then it occurred to me—these are things I can't will to happen, study up on, or determine to try out. Patience, selfless service, connection with God, mercy, and most of all GRACE are not "life skills" to implement after a seminar, but rather are outcomes of trials and anguish.

Someone asked me recently where the good was in suffering. I think I conjured up a lame answer that I thought sounded good, but now I know that the good in suffering cannot be gotten ANYWHERE else. When you are broken, really and truly broken, down to the ugly, whining, sniveling level…when you have nothing and not one scrap of strength left to pretend you have it together…grace can just happen. Your ego has temper-tantrummed itself into exhausted sobs, your personal agenda is torn to bits, your possessions seem ridiculous, and your worries are brought down to matters of existence. It is then, when you're lying too limp to fight, that Heaven sweeps you in its arms and rocks you gently into GRACE.

Your "goodness," "holiness," intelligence, good works, devotionals, and efforts had NOTHING to do with how you got there. I think the reason we're suffering so much at this moment is that Steve and I spent a lot of time and effort trying to make a difference so that we could feel better about ourselves…or somehow EARN God's love. We had the best of intentions, but we were missing the blessing. No one EARNS a parent's love…it's just there for the accepting. A tough concept for those of us in this achievement-oriented world. It seems that if we can't compete for it, be acknowledged and rewarded for it, we can't appreciate it. We always want to be special or better than someone else…to have something that others can't have. Where's the value in something universally offered? I will tell you.

I'm darn glad that God doesn't make us earn His love, because when I needed it most, I would have failed in obtaining it in my anger, impatience, and pathetic self-pity. So now it's out. Dirty laundry aired. Truth laid bare…and any misconceptions you had about the perfection of Steve and Jan (mostly Jan…Steve's still amazing) are shattered. It's time to lighten up on yourselves. Cut each other some slack. Stop trying to be wonderful, and just accept the love you feel you don't deserve.

That's what I'm gonna do, and maybe I'll even get a little sleep in there somewhere. Love you all, you deliciously imperfect miracles!

Thanks for listening. Jan

Hi all, I will keep this shorter today…you deserve it! We had our second round of chemo yesterday, and Steve tolerated it well. The local chemo team at Dr. G's office was as lovely and wonderful as ever—a homecoming we wished we'd never have to make. The three-hour treatment left him utterly exhausted though, so it took Mac, Dave, and me to get him in and out of the office, car, house…

Unfortunately, they will not be around to assist with the next one; however, the Ocean Pines rescue guys have stepped up and offered to help with all future transports! (The folks from Ocean Pines Vol. Fire Dept. have been so kind and generous—gathering and delivering supplies and manpower—thanks, guys!)

We go back today for a NeuL— shot to boost Steve's white blood count. Also, Dr. G ordered a new wheelchair and handicapped tag for the car—something I'd never even thought about but will surely come in handy in getting Steve to and from locations.

Pieces are falling into place with physical, speech, and occupational therapy teams, but the one missing element is word from Care First on home aide/care. I miss my old case manager who always returned her calls and always came through with the answers needed. Please pray specifically that our new case manager will take up our cause… My return to work depends upon her efforts.

The kids continue to mend from their violent virus, and we all slept through the night—Yippie! I can think clearly this morning! Now to get all our accumulated belongings picked up and stowed so that we can maneuver in this maze we now call home.

New Year's Revelation and Resolution: I realized that all my useless possessions create roadblocks for Steve's mobility. AHHHH… Is there a bigger metaphor in play here??? Hmm… perhaps a purge would be good for both body AND soul.

Thanks for reading, but even more, thank you for your prayers. When I get out of my own way, I see God at work in EVERYTHING—despite me.

Love you all, jan

ONCE IN A BLUE MOON

Happy New Year's Eve,

I thought about writing something profound for New Year's Day, but I'm out of profound and the day is not here yet! So, I will let my brain play without me for a few minutes today...I promise it will "play nice" (bad grammar intended):

I'm trying to imagine what you all are doing right now...some of you are getting ready to visit family or friends, some battling lines in the "newly revamped" security areas at airports, some of you are in the hospital with loved ones, some of you are cooking black-eyed peas, while others dance to their music... And some of you are deciding which dress to wear to the party tonight while your men wonder if they really even need those clean clothes at all...

It truly warms my heart to think of you doing happy things or caring for one another in tender little ways. It reminds me that all around, life is abounding...enduring...and that every dark night has its dawn.

Sometimes, that dark night can even surprise us with a BLUE MOON such as the one we enjoyed last night. It was almost time to put Steve to bed, and I was offering up a silent prayer to Bob (God) asking for strength to be better at taking care of Steve's needs, when through a little octagonal window on my stairway, there shone—like a beacon in a tempest—an unbelievably huge, perfectly round moon that illuminated the entire sky. I was transfixed…it was flawlessly centered in the window, wreathed in wispy clouds, and a little voice in my head said, *The darker the sky, the brighter I shine.*

I think our lives have been like that this past week. Dark, very dark at times, but in that darkness, your love, our love for each other, and the love our Heavenly Father showers on us can shine unimpeded without competition for our attention. Some of you mentioned that you were worried I was losing my faith, my resolve, but let me assure you that just the opposite has occurred.

When nights ran into days without sleep and I foundered in my duties as a caregiver, allowing worry to seep into my mind, you stepped in with your lovely flickering candles of love and dispelled the gloom. You may have thought your gestures small or ineffective but KNOW THIS—there is not enough darkness in all the world to extinguish the light of even a single candle.

Here are just a few of your little points of light that banished my darkest of nights. YOU:

- Offered/brought us medical supplies
- Ran to the store for food
- Helped me transport Steve to chemo
- Dropped food at my door
- Offered to host a fundraiser
- Wrote in our guestbook/email
- Brought coffee and donuts to Steve
- Checked up on disability benefits for us
- Offered to sub for me a little longer at school

- Baked cookies for Steve
- Made us a Christmas wreath
- Sent us something to help with our finances

So, instead slamming the door on a miserable year that ended badly, we can now say that 2009 was wonderful and 2010 will be even better! And, thanks to shining lights such as you, it doesn't just have to happen once in a BLUE MOON.

Loving you all to the moon and back,
Janni

HITTING THE ROCK

Greetings from 2010!

This is my first post of the year, and I would like to give a shout out to my friend Cris D, who is the caregiver child of two parents who've been struck down with brain tumors. When life seems unfair, just remember that everyone has a story...everyone his burden. Cris has more than most, but continues in a deep, abiding faith, taking time to uplift others. This 2010...I want to be more like Cris.

Okay, as I shared with Cris earlier, I found myself with a quiet moment after putting Steve in bed last night. I was too tired to clean, cook, or even read, so I vegged with the remote and surfed channels, stumbling on an amazing little drama about a monk in Montreal (named Brother Andre). This humble little man suffered terrible physical challenges, but he ended up taking care of and curing thousands of sick people. When asked why he couldn't cure his own physical ailments, he said, "They will always remind me of why I'm here and how these children suffer...then I offer up that suffering to God as the only gift I have to give. The pain never actually leaves, but somehow it has true meaning and I can bear it. The pain brings me closer to our Lord."

This suffering, which in our life now takes the shape of daily tasks, does act like a refiner's fire, searing and burning away what doesn't matter. As Cris said the other day, "When you hit rock bottom, that's when you find out who your rock is..." I know who our Rock is, and Steve is firmly rooted there and braces himself on it to get through his day. Our oncologist even said, as he hugged Steve after chemo, "Steve, old buddy, you fight harder than anyone I've ever known."

You see, a month ago, I didn't know that a simple shower could take at least an hour, that dressing could leave one breathless, and that climbing into bed could bring on a sweat, but that is the effort Steve must exert for simple daily tasks, and then only with assistance. He must gather himself to sit up, to struggle from couch to wheelchair, and to wince in determination to merely request a drink. Each time he does, I say a prayer of thanks for one more victory. Sometimes, he cries with frustration, apologizing to the air for his weakness, but most of the time he vows through gritted teeth, "I'm going to get better; I'm going to get better!" After a second brain tumor followed by a stroke, one could say that Steve has hit rock bottom, but I believe his Rock has given him the foothold to stand again.

So, it is but a small thing for me to offer up my discomfort, my fatigue, and interruptions to my easy lifestyle. I'm only the bystander to a miracle that Steve is grinding out with sheer will and belief in his healing. As a result, I resolve to rely less on my own limited strength, my finite patience, and feeble efforts and place my feet on my Rock and trust that it will hold fast in the shifting sands and buffeting waves of trials that we call life.

We'll leave the rest up to Bob—He knows what to do. We pray you hit your Rock too.

All love, jan and steve

Long day today, but much accomplished. We had blood draws first thing this morning, followed by a grueling physical therapy session. Then I got Steve shaved, showered, and gussied up—a process that leaves us both exhausted. Steve collapsed for a deep slumber while Mac and I took down and stowed all the Christmas decorations. Then later, we had to rouse Steve for his speech therapy appointment, but he was so tired he could barely sit up. I hope this means he'll sleep through the night!

It was bittersweet not being able to return to work today—bitter because I love my job and miss my students so much, and sweet because I could concentrate all my efforts on trying to ease things for Steve. I am praying hard about finding a solution to home care for Steve… I trust that God will help me resolve things as He's helped me with everything else so far. I want Steve to be comfortable, loved, and safe.

Often lately, keeping Steve safe involves changing the TV channel. Since everything that's happened, it seems that he can no longer stomach anything negative, violent, or depressing. He rolls his eyes at the 2012 doomsday predictions and shakes his head at arguing politicians. Often, we surf the channels until we find something funny or peaceful (which usually leaves *America's Funniest Home Videos*, *Planet Earth*, or *M*A*S*H*). When I commented to Steve on this new habit of ours, he said, "I have a big hole in my brain now…why would I want to fill it with garbage?" Good point, Steve…why would any of us?

I will admit that at first, I missed the latest breaking news stories, but truthfully, I am much calmer since I've been avoiding them along with disaster documentaries and shows about women who hate the way they look. I've even given up *WHAT NOT TO WEAR* as I recognize myself in every BEFORE shot. Pajamas ARE TOO day wear, Stacey and Clinton!!!!

So, days progress, Steve continues to work on regaining his strength, Mac continues to help, and I continue to learn about how to be a better person from my husband. I guess some things never change.

Oh, GOOD GRIEF! Cosmic Comedy...

Okay...I've had my belly-busting laugh for the day...and I feel better already! I was checking the Internet for in-home care people. I found a registry for home-companions in the area, and I clicked on several profiles claiming the standard abilities, compassion, care, etc... However, the fifth one stopped me in my tracks with its opening statement:

"My children are now grown, and I have done lots of jobs, waitress, office, and home care for a man which was great—until he died."

Once I stopped laughing (Mac and I were both in tears over this one), I decided that word-of-mouth referrals might be the better bet. I guess I'll get back on that phone.

Love to you all, and remember to laugh... Life is precious, especially when it's utterly ridiculous! janni

MIRACLE MAN RISES AGAIN!

So far, today has been a day of answered prayers, so I'll share while the good news is still fresh. Although we had a difficult night of wakefulness, each time we got up we used the walker— something we could barely manage yesterday. After we got up for the final time, Steve put on his shirt and sweater without assistance, brushed his own teeth, and walked to the couch with his walker. You must understand that this is a HUGE deal, as yesterday we could only take about six steps total.

Not to be outdone by his legs and arms, Steve's sense of humor stepped up its game as well. I handed him his morning meds with a glass of acai/pomegranate juice (usually his favorite), but I forgot that he'd just brushed his teeth. I realized how awful tart things can taste after toothpaste, but I realized it a little too late as Steve was swigging down a mouthful with his pills. What followed next could only be compared to the *Funniest Home Videos* of babies tasting something bitter for the first time. His eyes squinted shut, lips pursed, and tremors shook his whole body—a truly violent automatic response. With an incredulous look on his face, Steve then commented, "And I thought you LOVED me!"

We had a good laugh about that until his therapists arrived. The physical therapist was delighted with Steve's walking and measured that he'd walked fifty feet without help! Then the occupational therapist had him work with manipulating his hand. With his weak hand, Steve was able to fold and scrunch a dishtowel—remember that just last week it mostly hung limp. She was especially pleased when Steve finished his session by putting on his own socks! Both gals feel confident that Steve will make an excellent recovery, and their goal is to get him back in his wood shop!

This may be of little surprise to most of you as we all know Steve's resilience, but the timing could not have been more divine! Just last night I caught myself worrying about his progress, my return to work, etc. When I realized what I was doing, I had to actively turn it over to the big guy—BOB (Steve's way of saying God). I reminded Him that I was giving the burden over to Him since He always handles it better than I. I told Him that I would have faith that things would work out. I guess I just didn't expect it to happen so quickly!

Most of you would say that I shouldn't be surprised—Bob is all-powerful—and I would agree with you. But I cannot help but wonder if Steve didn't hear me read yesterday's caregiver profile out loud…you know…the one where the caregiver said she loved her job "until the man died" …hmmm. Perhaps that was just the motivation Steve needed to bounce back with such gusto!

May you all accomplish today's goals without the threat of a "killer companion"!

Jan

January 7, 2010

Lessons I learned today:

Here's a helpful household hint...if you're worried about slips and falls in your home, especially in your kitchen, just do what I did. Allow a bottle of ginger ale to explode and spray all your surfaces, and even if you wipe up, you'll still retain that helpful tacky quality that grips your slippers!

Another helpful exercise hint...if you find yourself getting sedentary, just grab a book and snuggle up on your couch. In no time at all, the phone will ring off the hook, requiring you to get up and check caller ID. You will answer promptly as it appears to be one of your doctors, but you'll quickly find that it is yet another medical marketing company asking questions about health concerns. Then you get to explain that you're amid your own health concerns. In no time you'll be invigorated by your race to the phone and by the swiftness of the hang-up on the part of your chagrined caller.

A healthy eating hint...if you are making healthy choices in your diet, just eat a seedless Clementine orange. The unexpected seed that is hiding there will chip your tooth, making it impossible to even consider such temptations as ice cream!

A final reality check hint...just when you begin rejoicing about the dinner some thoughtful friend provided, or the medical expense fund that was opened for you, or the lovely card your students made you, HOLD ON. The euphoria that threatens to distract you from your chores will not last.

No, if you just wait, a beloved relative will end up in the hospital, one of your children will call in tears, or your bank will call telling you they've been hacked and have deactivated all bank cards and you'll receive your new one within two weeks. And, if you wait another minute, your son will get sick and must stay elsewhere, your husband will be told that if he loses more weight he'll be fitted with a stomach tube, and the nurse will also inform you of his rising white count, signifying infection.

You see, by just attempting to pour a drink, read a book, eat some fruit, or rejoice over blessings, you can bring the house down upon your head!

Now seriously...you didn't think I would end an update with such cynicism, did you? Well, of course not. I am merely trying to illustrate an Old Testament truth about there being a season for everything under heaven. For every challenge I whined about above, there are far more blessings to offset. Besides...without those helpful little lessons, how would we begin to know what rest, goodness, comfort, and peace are?

So, thank you, Bob (God), for both the good and the bad... the happy and the sad...the solutions as well as the problems. Remember...the darker the sky, the brighter the moon. I guess you could say that the Universe is mooning me pretty good right now.

Ha ha, Bob, very funny!

Happy Snow Day!

We awoke to a winter won-
derland that covered the bleak
backyard under a blanket of
beauty.

I love this picture I just took
because you can't see all the un-
done chores such as un-weeded
flower beds, untended patio fur-
niture, and un-emptied planters. Snow does a wonderful job in
hiding the unsightly. To some it is a curse, but to us teachers who
are behind on our yard work it is a two-fold blessing. You see, on
the Eastern Shore of MD, an inch and a half of snow will effec-
tively bring life as we know it to a screeching halt—including the
closing of schools. Enjoy, my beloved colleagues!

Yes, snow is so wonderful that we can even use it as a model
for living! It's true! We can learn a lot from snow…namely, if it
ain't pretty, just cover lightly with snow for a new, improved look!
You know…a "snow job."

Here are some examples of SNOW JOBS FOR LIFE:

PRE-SNOW		SNOW JOB:
Stretchy pants	=	petroleum-based yoga attire
Twinkies for breakfast	=	insulin instigation modules

Bed-head hair	=	a tousled pixie
Sprawling on the couch	=	rejuvenate posturing
Channel surfing	=	digitized dexterity training
Catalogue browsing	=	marketing demographic research
Snoring where you sit	=	audible somnambulism
Drooling while you snore	=	hydro-decibels
Microwaving leftovers	=	molecular stimulation recycling
Eating meals over the sink	=	logistical sustenance maximization
Reading my boring blogs	=	charitable indulgence

See what you can learn on a snow day? May your day be filled with cups of hot chocolate, good books, and loved ones in jammies under blankets. Turn off the phones and lock the doors and don't let anyone see your new SNUGGIE…no, make that a PERSONAL TEMPERATURE REGULATION POD. Either way, keep it to yourself.

Now…back to the couch, and junk food, and the remote!

Of Hearth and Home

Daughter Heather has come for a few days, and we have thoroughly enjoyed her company. Daughter Candy is doing medical duty for Steve's dad, who is in the hospital as I write—thanks, Can, we miss you though! Please pray that Dad Jack makes a swift recovery.

Anyway, we three had a cozy in-home day by the fire with Maryland crab soup bubbling on the stove. We watched and giggled at old comedies, bundled up together on the couch, and made milkshakes (all to inspire Steve to eat more of course). It was as normal a day as we've had in a while, and this afternoon I even felt comfortable enough to head out to Walmart—wow wee.

It's interesting…everyone keeps telling me I need to get out or get a break, but I don't think people truly understand. Yes, there are times when I feel as if I do nothing but fetch drinks, food, blankets, meds, wheelchair…and occasionally I find myself impatient or frustrated when we can't sleep through the night or when I can't accurately decipher what Steve is trying to say. However, I wasn't at Walmart ten minutes before I was mentally rushing the woman cutting my three yards of fabric or wishing the checker would hurry with the scanner so that I could get back home.

On the way back, I even realized that a breather is nice, but being with my husband—even when he's confused or frustrated with his challenges—is about the nicest thing in the world. I couldn't wait to get to hug him, kiss his thin face, hold his head in my lap, and stroke his thinning hair while he sleeps. While the world spins on and life dances by, I am content to spend my moments this way.

A friend of mine (who has lost the love of her life to this awful disease) helped me see that each moment should be savored, and that any chance to snuggle with my hubby should be grasped. Steve makes it easy though…even when he's too weak to sit up or speak, he'll blow me a kiss and mouth the words "I love you." Often, he'll even ask, "Are you okay? Can I get you anything?" out of habit. Oh, that all our habits were like that.

Well, the sun has set, we've put Steve to bed, and Heather, Mac, and I are laughing over *King of the Hill*. We do miss Candy, son-in-law Mike, Chelsea, and Dave, but we are truly enjoying this time together. I think this is one of those days where the moon outshines the night! (Reference earlier posts if you're confused.)

Thanks, Bob…I'm getting to like this mooning business. May you all enjoy such quiet, achingly normal moments…and see them for the treasures they are.

with love, jan

Hi All,

This will hopefully be short and sweet…well, at least not too sour. The Bible says, "Ask and it shall be given, seek and ye shall find, knock and it shall be opened unto you." Okay…I'm askin':

I could use a hand fixing a cabinet in my kitchen that holds our trash cans. You see, when I opened it tonight to remove the bins, the whole drawer dropped, and a thousand ball bearings skittered across the kitchen. You'd have thought the ginger ale from earlier this week would have slowed them down, but no… they scattered like dogs at the sight of a vacuum.

While we're at it…does anyone know how to grout a few tiles and install a hand-grab bar? I'm doing my best to cover all the bases, but I don't have time to go to Home Depot for training in some of these areas. I'd like to draw on existing expertise. Glenn (Steve's paramedic partner) might be making us a wheelchair ramp, so he may need a crew as well—we'll keep you updated. (I can offer pizza, soda, chips, whatever, and Steve will comment on your progress!)

Therapy and the heavy-duty chemo continue this week, so we'll need extra happy thoughts and prayers. One thing we're very excited about is having our friend Father Duffy from the fire department serve us Holy Communion on Wednesday. This should be a special time and create a wonderful memory.

Again, I thank all of you for your wonderful cards, emails, thoughts, visits, food, and gifts. We are humbled by your generosity and loving care, and we pray for you all each day. If you have questions, suggestions, or manual skills, drop me an email or write in the guestbook. Also, if you need special prayer for anyone or anything, let us know. That's something we can still do these days.

Thanks, and know that no matter what falls apart, Bob is still in charge. BOB (God) bless you, Janni

Do you speak *Stephenese*?

Chelsea and Dave returned today after nine days in Philly and noticed a DISTINCT improvement in Steve! YAY! Even though he's still speaking "Stephenese" (as Mac calls it), he's easier for them to understand. Steve had to call it an early evening, though, because he was exhausted. We had physical therapy, occupational therapy, a visit from our colleague Jenn, buddy Phil, and neighbor Jim-the-builder.

We started the day well with a call from a contractor hired for us by an anonymous angel, and the contractor will be here on Thursday for a day of "chores." Whoever you are that is sending this handyman—you are truly a guardian angel! I cannot thank you enough!!!! Then, the emails from sweet folks who want to help with the ramp-building, grouting, etc. began to pour in, and the scriptural promise of blessings "pressed down, shaken, and overflowing" was made manifest. Thanks, Bob (the Master Builder).

During Jim-the-builder's visit, what began as a request for a grab-bar installation turned into plans for a whole bathroom renovation…we're just not equipped for someone with a walker, let alone a wheelchair. My bathroom door is narrower than twenty-eight inches, and I must straddle the toilet to get Steve in the shower. This will be a good move for our future. Thanks, Jim-the-builder, for making it happen for us! Also, when we build the ramp, I will announce the day and time for all of you volunteers!

I hope to replace the downstairs carpet as well with something less squishy. Watching Steve try to wheel or walk across is painful—like pushing a wagon through sand. I will look for a good deal on a commercial grade, extremely flat carpet—hardwood is not in our stars at this point. We also looked at traffic patterns in the house, and we'll be moving furniture tomorrow. Jim-the-builder's functional eye truly helped because I've been unable to see solutions from looking too hard…kind of like the ketchup bottle staring you in the face on the top shelf of the fridge while you stand there gaping.

The generous donations you have sent will go directly to bills and paying for the retrofitting of our home for Steve's medical needs. It really surprised me that none of it is covered whatsoever by insurance. They'll patch you up, give you drugs, but then you're on your own. No complaints though; we are lucky and blessed to have insurance at all. If you don't believe me, Steve's ONE chemo treatment at Duke with visit to Brain Tumor Clinic was $26,000.00 per infusion because we're on the clinical trial. I just wonder what in the world folks do without insurance. I will pray extra hard for them.

Also, please pray for Steve's dad, Jack, as he's having a pacemaker put in tomorrow. It really upsets Steve not to be at his dad's side for this as we've always done in the past. Steve knows Dad's in good hands with his brother Mike and daughter Candy, but it's not the same as being there in person. I can relate as I haven't been able to visit my mom in the Alzheimer's unit since December 1st. The only blessing is that she doesn't seem to know us anymore, so she doesn't know that I haven't been there. I really wish I had her here and whole, so I could talk to her. She was always so good in crisis situations and taking care of us when we were sick. It's a time like this that I really hate what Alzheimer's has stolen from us and her. My thoughts are turning inward—one day at a time, Jan. Perhaps it is time to call my brother, Dan (the shrink); he's a good listener as well as being great with our mom. (Okay, that thought will make me start crying.)

You know…I was thinking about the meaning of the Lord's Prayer, which so many of us can recite in our sleep. For all the years I've spoken it, I never TRULY examined it. Today, the line "Give us this day our daily bread" finally became clear to me. Bob (God) never promises that we'll win the lottery or make windfall profits, but He DOES offer daily sustenance…to meet our daily needs. I realized that if I put forth the need and get out of the way, Bob goes to work organizing the fulfillment of that need. If He were to give us a fortune all at once, we might not think we need Him again, pious in our "financial security." Bob also reminded us to "consider the lilies of the valley…they neither toil nor sweat, but Solomon in all his glory was never arrayed as one of these."

Translated to STEPHENESE… Fret not…fear not…Bob's got your back…what else do you need? Now go live your day fearlessly! All love, jan

January 14, 2010

Message from Steve

Good morning. Wanted to write before the chaos and mayhem begins. Have a carpenter, nurse, and three therapists coming in today, so this will most likely be the only free moment I have. Quick note—yesterday, we had Communion with Father Duffy—a very special moment…and Steve was completely fluent with the Lord's Prayer—thank you, Father D.

Well, when Steve heard what we have on the plan for the day, he wasn't pleased. He sighed and hung his head, knowing how much of his effort it would take. I got him settled on the couch with the news and promised him coffee, but when I returned, he was in tears.

I assumed it was the heavy schedule, but he VERY QUICKLY and very articulately told me why he was crying. "I'm so upset… look at those poor suffering people… I wish I was better so that I could go there and help them." It took me a minute to realize it wasn't a bad dream or incoherent rambling. He reached both arms out and pulled me into a bear hug. He cried against me for a moment, until I asked, "What people, honey?"

"Them!" and he pointed over my shoulder. I turned to see the graphic TV footage from Haiti of their devastating earthquake. There was a sobbing father carrying a child, and a husband desperately tearing apart his shack, looking for his wife. Steve held me harder and cried, "I can hold you, but he can't find his wife…I'm so lucky." We held each other in our safe, warm home, knowing where our loved ones were. Things may be stretched and strained, but we have food, shelter, health care, and love.

When I sat to write this, Steve said, "All I want you to tell them (you all) is pray for the people of Haiti...we all come from Bob (God)."

So...please pray for our brothers and sisters in Haiti, Steve's dad and the new pacemaker, and for those who are wounded and healing, physically and spiritually.

And, we'll pray for you. Jan

Momentary Chill (I wrote this poem just after driving home from chemo treatment)

The holly bears witness to withering woods and fading fields.
It watches curled leaf drop to carpet of discarded needles
while grapevine swoons lifeless against cypress.
It sees the cattail blow itself apart spilling seed brains
all over the wilting water bush.
The only sound—death rattle of corn husk
and last gasp of wasted mum croaking, "All is lost…"
The holly stands sentry to enshrouding silence…and
sits vigil over winding sheets of white.
Its grief betrayed only by blood red tears
shed for the notion of mortality,
carried off by the careless robin.
But the holly understands resurrection…
It has viewed evidence of rebirth
and wondrous restoration.
For what now lies wretchedly barren will spring forth again.
No matter how clever the tomb…
how convincing the grave…
nothing truly dies forever.

Yesterday, while driving home from the hospital where Steve got his NeuL— shot, we were struck by the ice that still rings the trees in the woods along the road. Everywhere were shades of gray and brown with touches of white. It was hauntingly beautiful, but somber, reflecting our dark days of fatigue and weariness. Miles of muted colors passed until we crossed the Pocomoke River and the first holly trees came into view. They alone stood green in the barren woods, and I was reminded that there is always life...and hope...even in the desolation of winter.

Chemo took about five hours on Friday, leaving Steve exhausted, but sleep would elude us. Nausea and nervousness brought on by the drugs kept Steve awake and weakened him. This morning, while he tried to push himself by using his walker more and wheelchair less, Steve had his first fall since the stroke. Luckily it was on carpet, but he was stunned and shaken, and he cried as I struggled to get him off the floor. He was upset that he had to be lifted and kept apologizing. It broke my heart, because in his brokenness, he worried about me. But that is Steve.

We kept the anti-nausea meds going, and he was able to have his milkshakes. Today promises to be a better day as my brother and sister-in-law are coming. It will be fun to have new faces who bring helping hands. So, they will be the holly in our woods... along with all of you and your delicious chicken soup, dip, roast beef, potato salad, cookies, cards, angels, visits, generous gifts, prayers, and your love.

Thank you for reminding us that life prevails.
All love, jan

Howdy!

We slept through the night and I am giving thanks!!!! As I try to figure out why, I consider the possibility of Steve's outing yesterday with son-in-law Dave, who wheeled Steve in the sun for quite a while. Or, perhaps it was the yummy dinner he ate in its entirety last night with a milkshake chaser! Or maybe it was the hour of occupational therapy where his fine motor skills were tested and found to be improving. Or maybe it was all your loving prayers. Whatever the reason, it was a Bob-send (FYI—Steve's word for God is Bob).

I think maybe the feel of the house is lighter as I am purging things to make room for Steve's maneuvers. I took bags full of books to the library, and piles of clothing to the thrift shop. I've been on an organization rampage since reading that de-cluttering improves a patient's recovery time. It is grueling, but it feels wonderful letting so much unnecessary stuff go—why did I ever think I needed a rice-cooker in the first place?

Now I even think I'm ready to tackle my art studio/bonus room, but it is so daunting I might need backup. Any of you fancy yourselves as a clutter coach? Even just having someone hold the bag while you purge is nice. My sister-in-law Peggy did that for me this weekend, and her encouragement meant the world. Brother Kent kept Steve occupied so that I could do it…otherwise Steve gets nervous if I'm not within eyesight or earshot.

Well, here's to a happy, quiet, and better day. I know that tough days lie ahead, but what a difference a night's sleep can make. Ya know, until this struggle of late, I needed bigger and bigger signs from God to let me know I'm blessed. Perhaps my life was so filled with stuff and activity, I missed the simple gifts. So, a good night's sleep is my "daily bread" for today. That's all I was told to expect, and somehow, that's really all we need.

Have a lovely day and remember to look for your "daily bread." Hugs, jan

January 21, 2010

Hi Everyone,

I guess little blessings can turn into bigger ones...especially when we're not looking! Yesterday was a flurry of activity and surprises with physical therapy, blood draws, and visits from Steve's "adopted" son, paramedic Larry, and the manager of Taylor Bank.

Now, a visit from a bank manager could be an intimidating thing, but this one turned out to be anything but. He showed up to get our signatures on a new fund that loving friends have set up for Steve to help with expenses and handicap access. Steve was so overwhelmed he burst into tears, and when Steve's partner, Glenn, told the manager how many people Steve has helped or taught or mentored over the years, the bank manager cried too.

Steve kept saying, over and over, "I just can't believe this...I didn't do anything special...why me?" Now the amazing thing is that never once in two years of tumors, brain surgery, and treatments has Steve ever asked, "Why me?" Only when folks pour out their love, he asks, and that deep humility answers the question.

After the bank manager left, Steve asked me again why people had set up a fund. I told him that they loved him and wanted him to have a safe bathroom, or for us to be able to pay our electric bill, or just help with expenses while I am on leave. His whole face lit up and he said, "You mean you get to stay with me and take care of me a little longer?" And when I assured him that I would, he broke down and sobbed.

"Don't you want me to stay home with you?" I asked.

"I do, I do…I was afraid you were going to leave me home with a babysitter…and I'm not ready yet…I just want you for now." The innocence, the vulnerability, and the raw honesty of his fear tugged at my heart and I knew I had made the right, albeit tough, decision to stay with him. I just put it all in Bob's (God's) hands, and He sent us a bank account.

If I never receive another thing in my life, I know that I have had more than my share of blessings, and it does my heart good to see Steve receiving his. Bob is good.

In our weakness, He is strong…in our brokenness, He mends, and in our darkest night, He lights the way. May you turn it over to Bob today and know that you are in good Hands.

We love you all, Steve and jan

At the request of neighbors, family, and friends (and in my prideful discomfort) here is the info: Steve Calloway Fund: XXXXXX

January 22, 2010—Chemo Dip in the Roller Coaster of Life

Hi there. It has been one full week since Steve's hard-core chemo, and it is really hitting him. They said that one to two weeks after chemo would be the toughest as his white cell counts drop, and he is huddled in my lap as I write—it's a balancing act with computer on my right knee and Steve's head on my left. I snuggled him under his warming blanket, but he's still shivering.

The folks who stopped by today got to say hi, but Steve's emotions were brimming over (as were his tears), and I could tell their heartstrings were plucked. The ravaging fatigue that is a byproduct of chemo wears down his defenses, and everything seems too much—the good as well as the bad.

Steve ate well, and he loved the goodies cooked and brought over by two of my lovely students and their mom. Their shining faces touched Steve, and he was once again awed by the kindnesses shown. My gal pal teachers also pitched in to provide a grocery shop, and they added many thoughtful items that weren't even on the list, but which were most helpful—again delivered with warm hugs and beaming smiles.

The thoughtfulness of others abounds. I dare anyone to say that Americans are greedy, that today's youths are selfish, that people are too busy to care for others. If you identify with that group, please, come to my house and watch the miracle of true human nature unfold.

I reject the notion of man's inhumanity to man with every brownie that walks through our door...with every errand neighbors run...with every nail in our ramp...with every card, email, and phone call to say we're loved. I embrace Anne Frank's assertion that people are basically good—she would love my neighbor who brings meals over in a little red wagon and the kids who take the time to send me daily messages on the Internet.

People ARE good...they WANT to be good...and they are so blessed by BEING good. It took me a while to ask for help as Steve and I were the ones who enjoyed giving it, but when I did, I opened the floodgates of goodness and Bob's (God's) love poured out and washed over our household. People seem eager, willing, and ready to help. They bring things by with such joy and happy spirit that I know that true goodness just waits for the chance to spring forth!

So, the next time you're cut off by a reckless speeder on the highway, or when you hear the impatient sigh of the person behind you at the checkout line, or when you get the server who forgot she's there to SERVE, send them each a silent prayer of mercy. They are in the small minority who is missing out on all that joy. They need your loving pity rather than your scorn. Just smile, send them love, and go make those brownies!

And wish my baby boy, Mac, a big Happy 21st Birthday... we cannot forget to celebrate living!!!!

We love you all, Steve and jan and Biggum Boy Mac

Good morning, Lord!!! (not good Lord, it's morning…)

Today will be a better day. Steve's digestive system seems to be straightening out, so perhaps he'll be more comfortable and able to eat more. We haven't slept well for several nights now, but he's finally in a deep sleep on his beloved couch with his pillow and head on my lap. Again, I type on my right knee, so heaven only knows what typos there'll be.

I guess we'll shave Steve's head today. He wanted to see what he would look like with a little hair, so I haven't shaved his head in over a month. He grew the softest little covering of down that I often stroke to soothe him when the bad moments come, but this morning, I noticed that it is falling out in my fingers. That is too much for him to watch and bear, so we'll take care of it today.

I am hoping he'll be comfortable enough at home with son-in-law, Dave, so that I can go get my "chemo cut" today. Yes, that's what my stubby haircut is officially called by the gals at the Hair Cuttery. It began two years ago as my way of showing that Steve I didn't care that he was bald, but we both liked it so much that it stuck! Many folks urge me to grow it out, but true love looks beyond appearances anyway. Imagine my surprise, though, when my students showed up in class last year with the same cut in honor of Steve! How wonderful they are!!!

I just realized that today is about one month since Steve's stroke, and when I begin to wonder if we'll ever graduate from wheelchair to full-time walker I simply must look back. One month ago, to-day, Steve was in a hospital bed, barely moving his right arm and leg, unable to speak, and unable to follow instructions or commands. However, within just one month, he can walk a bit with his walker, transfer himself in and out of his wheelchair, brush his teeth, use his electric shaver, feed himself, and talk so that I can understand him most of the time. Even better, all his therapists feel he's making continuing improvement. All while his tumor shrinks!!

The therapists remind me all the time that he works harder than most stroke patients, and he is doing it with the added burden of chemo for a brain tumor. All in all—a Herculean task.

And, in that month, we've gotten a ramp, received wonderful meals, and we're on our way to being able to afford to renovate our bathroom for Steve. While each item seems but an incremental step, when seen in the whole, miracles are taking place.

I used to call Steve my Miracle Man, but now I think I need to amend that. Steve is the Miracle Magnet! He has this almost divine ability to bring out the best in others, to show them how to be their highest selves, and to trust in a loving, caring Father who never forsakes them. Well…that's at least what he's done for me, so I guess he's still my Miracle Man too.

We hope you enjoy your Sunday. We pray this update finds you happy, well, and perhaps getting much-needed rest, but my wish for you today is that you let go of needless worry: get your focus off your wardrobe, your looks, your possessions, your accomplishments, and your status. Trust me—these things are empty, fleeting, and false—but your relationship with your loved ones and your Maker—now that is where your true treasure lies.

Good morning, Lord!!!!

UPDATE ON JAN'S DENTAL SAGA:

Two weeks ago, I chipped my tooth on a seed in a "seedless" Clementine... After repairs, I enjoyed days of comfort until...

Today. I chipped the same tooth on a cucumber.

Moral of Story:

Stick to ice cream.

Water, water everywhere but ne'er a drop to drink…

Hi gang. Yesterday was a bit of a challenge. Steve was considerably dehydrated, and his blood pressure kept dipping to the point that our physical therapist declined to work him out. Steve's insistence on only coffee and avoidance of all things water caught up with him at last. We have consistently pushed fluids—water, juices, and Gatorade, but Steve has resisted; however, a stern talking-to by nurses put the fear of Bob in him.

Today, he's drinking everything we're offering, and his BP is better, but his pulse rate is still high, so we'll have to monitor that. Also, his white counts were through the roof, so I told Duke docs that I thought the NeuL— shots were overkill. They agreed, so we'll forego it this week and see what happens.

Occupational therapy is here right now, and I can tell by her reactions that Steve's hand strength and mind/muscle memory are returning. Last night's speech therapy was encouraging as well, so we're once again offering prayers of thanks.

We had so many wonderful visits and food surprises yesterday, and Steve always worries we'll forget to thank everyone properly. We try to assure him that you all know just how much your thoughtfulness means to us and how much we love you and feel loved BY you. Sometimes he grows very tired and even sleeps when you come over, but we know you understand and don't take it personally. He wants to be sure that you don't.

Thank you for praying for us. I cannot tell you how much it

means to Steve's healing. The medicine and docs are tools, but divine intervention and intention are the hands of the Craftsman… and together, we're forging a marvelous healing—not only Steve's body, but our souls and hearts as well. Thank you for being a part of our team, and we hope you're being blessed too. My prayer list grows longer each day, but I am honored that you've entrusted me with your concerns…please feel free to keep doing so.

Praying for you, jan and steve

Hakuna Matata!

Hope this update finds you tucked up on the couch in your SNUGGIES! We are pretty much sofa spuds right now, drawing straws to see which

one must go to the trouble of clicking the remote or flipping the switch on the gas fireplace.

We're a regular little African safari at siesta time around here... Steve's like a baby gazelle—all knees and wobbles—dozing after a strenuous day of learning to walk. Son-in-law Dave is a worn-out jackal—sprawling in the big chair—paws draped off the edge of the ottoman, licking his chops after another great dinner, which leaves me—Miss Hippo—lumbering across the room to plop down in my spot, eyes peeking above the surface of the blanket, having just eaten my bodyweight in gourmet ice cream sent by a concerned friend worried about my chipped tusk. Even Darcy, Dave and Chelsea's puppy, is begging food from a prone position.

As you might surmise...my mind is playing without me. You could say I'm dancing in delirium. It often happens when I'm over-tired and under-napped. I've had to do more than a lot of translating today...from Stephenese to English. Steve is clearly benefitting from the positive effects of rehydration, which tends to make him hungrier and chattier. Dave has been a marvelous steward, taking turns with me in answering Steve's continuous requests for food or drink, but he's needed some translations. Dave's picking up the language quickly though and now knows the Stephenese for "May I have some pudding?" Stephenese: Can I have the stuff you take out and go like that and eat all over up to here? (pointing to his mouth)

I believe tomorrow Dave will master the Stephenese for "May I have some coffee/hot chocolate?" Stephenese: May I have some warm boat for here? We laugh, repeat it in English for Steve to see if we have it right, and fetch the desired goody. When visitors come, their looks of complete bafflement at these exchanges are rather entertaining.

It's much funnier now that Steve realizes that he's mixing things up. We can even laugh about it together. He knows immediately that he's said something twisted but can't always get it right. Case in point—after Dave and I had gotten him some dinner, Steve said, "Thank you, girls!" We laughed, and I said, "Hey, Dave, you're just ever so perty..." Steve caught on to what he'd done and said, "No, not girls...I meant ladies..."

Well, my fingers are getting exhausted...they're having to lift their own body weight with each word typed, so I think I'll let them take five...like the rest of me. Clearly, we're eating more and better than we've ever done—thank you, wonderful chef friends. Now... which one of you wants to be Miss Hippo's weight-loss coach?

A wink and a nod (any more is just toooo much work).

Love from Miss Cleopatra Hippo, Queen of "Denial," signing off for now

(get it, brothers Kent and Dan? Queen of de Nile???? Oh, never mind, I'll explain later, sigh.)

Hi there everyone,

Happy Friday! No chemo for Steve today…rescheduled for Monday, so he took an extra-long nap and enjoyed the quiet. I took that opportunity to sort through and shred old files, because it's amazing how quickly they pile up! I'm doing my best to keep up with my de-cluttering campaign. (Peggy, where are you???? And sorry, brother Mike, no luck on that file we're looking for.)

We're awaiting the return of son, Mac, from New York—we hope he beats the snow. We're only expected to get about two inches, but on the Eastern Shore of MD, that's grounds for becoming shut-ins. The bread's been flying off the shelves, and people are slugging it out over milk. Yep…the riot police have already staked out Food Lion, and I've even got my broom ready to clear all that snow off the steps…veritably, a Swiffer might do the job.

Good news on the med front. We're lowering Steve's steroid dose by half, and he's really looking forward to a reduction in side effects. Those on dexamethasone know what I'm talking about. The goal is getting off it completely, so we'd love your prayers for that.

I just have to add one thought—well, two. Within the past few days, quite a few of you have commented on my "strength" through this latest ordeal. First, I was always one of those people who dreaded the notion of becoming a caregiver—I never thought I could begin to do such a job. I would often marvel at the folks who looked after loved ones and wondered as to the secret of their dedication. Well, I think I have discovered it: there's really nothing to it. No major skill, no special knowledge, no extra measure of grace...just love. Take heart, dear ones, should you ever find yourself in such a position, relax and know that you will be okay. All you need to do is love with all your heart, and the rest just falls into place.

Second, "things falling into place" has a lot to do with a wonderful support system. I can be Steve's caregiver because of the caregiving YOU all provide. You cook for us, help us clean, get our mail, take out our trash, help us get to chemo, build us a ramp, send us email, cards, books, and gifts, come to visit, and most important—pray for us. With all that help, how COULD I fail?

So, the next time you wonder at my "strength," simply look in the mirror. Next to God, YOU are my strength...and for that I am forever grateful.

All love, jan

And the match goes to STEVE and Team Positive!!!!

The following was written exactly as dictated from Steve:

HI…Surprise!!! It's me!!! Just wanted to say hi, and good to see everybody. I'm fine and stuff…every day with my woman (he points to me)! I love to watch her tell funny stories. I'm excited to see her every day, and I love to tease her when she's not looking. Sometimes I get mixed up, but if I wait long enough I get it done right. Thanks for helping her, guys. I love her, and she makes me better. Oh, tell them I'm stirrin' it up! (Now distracted by the hat-making process on TV show How It's Made.*) Oh, I love that hat! I know, I'm being silly… Okay, that's all.*

Well so much for his talking about how he's doing. Steve made me read it back to be sure I didn't edit. I told him I was a bit embarrassed that he talked about me, and he said, "That's the most important thing, so tough! You're my sweetheart."

I debated whether to send this, but he doesn't ask much, and I promised he could say whatever he wanted…besides…why should being loved by one's husband be embarrassing? I feel so lucky, and I wish everyone could be loved like this by another human.

Chemo went relatively well today. We didn't have the highly toxic CARBO, so it was less debilitating and of shorter duration. Steve sat by the window and remarked over and over how lovely the snow was and how the sun sparkled on its surface. It was almost peaceful except for a patient who was wallowing in her own misery and determined to try to bring us down with her. She hadn't reckoned on Steve and me, and our nurse laughingly told her to forget it…she'd met her match in each of us!

The woman pitied herself loudly for having cancer, for having to go through treatment, for having to stay at home…you name it, but you all would have been so proud of Steve. He said, "You give cancer too much credit…it's not that strong." He then told her that he felt lucky they had medicine for it and that he had a home to rest in. Then he closed his eyes and said toward her, "Okay, no more," and promptly went to sleep.

Frustrated, she turned on me next… asked if I felt cheated by having to care for a "terminally ill" husband at my "tender age." I told her, "We're all terminal, and no, I consider caring for my husband to be a sacred honor." She guffawed and said, "Yeah, right."

I just smiled and replied, "Well, I do…I guess that just makes me weird." She asked about our jobs and asked bluntly how we could possibly manage with me on unpaid leave and him on disability. I considered shoving my Fiber One bar in her gob, but that would be a waste of good roughage, so I inhaled deeply (tried to remember that she's a hurting pup herself) and responded, "Ya know, it's funny…God never promised to make us wealthy, but He promised us our daily bread. I had toast today for breakfast, and it was pretty good, and we haven't been hungry yet." I then smiled, took out my book, and ignored her.

Before long, a new man arrived and was seated in a treatment chair. In no time she went to work on him too. Without knowing her modus operandi, however, he said, "Oh my, it's a beautiful day, isn't it?! God gave us that pretty snow, and I had a great cup of coffee on the way in!" Her jaw dropped, she shook her head in disgust, crossed her arms, put on her sunglasses, and sulked for the rest of her treatment… I believe the technical term for the end of any wrestling match where the loser is rendered impotent is "PIN!" and I could swear I heard Bob smack the mat.

February 3, 2010

Extreme Soul Makeover

I've been crying a lot today...each time for a different reason, so warning...this is lengthy.

Our day began sometime in the middle of the night. Often, after a round of chemo, Steve's nights are filled with restless energy. He has nightmares, tossing and turning, needing multiple bathroom runs. He also flails in his sleep, unconsciously smacking me in the face with his weak arm as he attempts to hug me. At first it was alarming, but I quickly realized what he was trying to do, so now I gently slide his arm around my waist and try to fall back to sleep (without much success).

So, that said, we are tired. Morning came too fast today, and when I tried to get us ready, I seemed to be all thumbs—banging the wheelchair into walls, cracking my head on a cabinet, and slicing my finger open with a chef's knife. Fatigue leads to stupidity, apparently, and I continued to mess up some other stuff not worth mentioning, but those dumb little things made me shed a few frustrated tears.

Steve was very weak today, struggling to maneuver. We struggled in the bathroom as his balance was off, and I fought to keep him from falling into the shower. He trembled as we got dressed and collapsed on the couch. Appetite was sketchy, and we spilled a lot—as a result, I discovered that couch pillows can survive the washer. So, it was midday before I could get my shower, and when I stepped in, I couldn't even bring myself to move aside Steve's shower chair. Somehow that felt like a betrayal, so I wedged up against the stall wall, washed my hair, and cried again.

After lunch, the physical therapist noted how weakened Steve was, and she also called my attention to how closely our daughter's dog watches over Steve. She commented on how it's been studied that dogs are hyper-sensitive to chemo patients. Later, I looked up those studies on the Internet, and what she hadn't mentioned was the reason that the dogs hover near chemo patients is that dogs sense the patient is closer to mortality and hence are standing vigil.

I went out to retrieve the mail today and found an ad for Colonial Williamsburg in Virginia. That reminded me that we had scheduled a trip there in December to celebrate our fifth anniversary until Steve had his stroke. I wondered if or when we would ever return, or if we would even have a sixth, and yes, there were tears for special "together moments" lost.

I sucked it up, went inside, and began to query Steve about dinner. It took him close to ten minutes to let me know that he wanted Scrapple (an Eastern Shore delicacy). He tried so hard to make me understand, and Dave did his best to decipher along with me. Finally, Steve managed the word "brown" and I got it. We were all brought to tears of relief. How horrible to not be understood when your requests are so very simple.

Then I read a bunch of emails and notes from friends and fellow caregivers, but the words "terminal" and "brain tumor" were linked so often that the enormity of brain cancer's prognosis factor was inescapable. Somehow, I guess I just refuse to think about mortality. Not denial, just optimism, but today my defenses are fragile, and I cried when I remembered that my husband has BRAIN CANCER, and this type of brain cancer is almost always incurable.

After dinner, Steve fell asleep on my lap and I turned on *Extreme Home Makeover* where they modified a home for a soldier amputee. My eyes began to well up, thinking about my daughter and son-in-law in the army, but mostly for the wounded soldiers to whom my students and I were writing and sending care packages. I've tried to keep up the correspondence and make things to send, but I've slacked lately—to my dismay and shame.

As the show unfolded, they demonstrated how difficult it was for the wounded soldier to maneuver around the house, and my heart broke for him...then I realized that we were in a similar situation. Here was my husband, who was so vital, so strong, and so active, curled up like a small child in my lap. His life is lived between bed and couch, and we have yet to make it through the bedroom door without hitting the jambs with the chair or walker. Showers are contortionist acts, and the wheelchair doesn't fit in the kitchen—no matter anyway—he cannot wheel himself for the weakness in his arm.

These limitations don't seem so bad when the weather is crummy outside, but Steve is a man of the outdoors. What will he do when spring arrives? He loves his flowers and vegetable gardens. Yard work, up to now, had been such a source of quiet pride with him and something at which he is so gifted. It had served to give him pleasure and purpose when he couldn't work, important when he couldn't work as a paramedic. Now that I sense he's beginning to realize that he won't EVER be able to work as a paramedic again since he cannot speak clearly or even drive, he would naturally consider his garden—a substitute passion; however, when he strains to use a walker on carpet, how will he even begin to negotiate a grassy yard?

The deck and front porch have stairs, so they're off limits now, and he can't stand long enough to enjoy his woodworking shop. He took up basket-weaving (yes, the man could do it all) after the first tumor, but the stroke has robbed him of the coordination to even do that.

I know I should be eternally grateful to have my husband at all, and I should be thankful to have this lovely home, but I'm beginning to resent its levels and tight corners. I've even pondered selling it to build a little bungalow outfitted for a handicapped person…but I know that would be too much for him right now.

And that reminded me that I have a tough choice. Either go back to work, leave Steve with sitters, and use the income to pay them and refit this house for new needs (and future needs), or stay put, manage the angles and corners as we have been doing, and stay home to continue caring for him.

You see, I am aware of the possibilities and realities that we might face. There is every possibility that God will work another miracle for Steve and heal him completely, and I am holding on to that. However, God may have other plans as well. If that's the case, I want to give my husband the best life I possibly can for as long as I can. I want to be the one who helps him up, the one who brings him meals, who cleans him up, shaves his head, washes his face, and holds him in my lap and lets him know he's adored. I want to savor every sweet moment we have for as long as we have. I want to be here when he laughs at *Funniest Home Videos* or when he calls out for me after a scary dream.

So, you see...while I am optimistic, while I love and adore God and have complete faith that He'll watch over us, I also have my limited human emotions. I don't want to lose my husband. I'm not ready to say good-bye.

Thank you for listening to my heart-strings playing a song of sad, self-pity. I wasn't going to share this, but if you're following along this path with us, you need to understand the WHOLE of it. Trials can be overcome, but they're not always easy. It would be irresponsible of me to pretend otherwise.

So, as I finish this up, Steve stirs, watches a few minutes of *Extreme Home Makeover*, and sighs. I ask him if he is okay, and he says, indicating the wounded soldier, "I wish I could help them with his house and make it better for him." The irony smacks me like a two-by-four. Here I am fretting over minor inconveniences, forgettable aches and pains, worrying about personal heartbreak and loss, while Steve, never giving such thoughts one ounce of energy, expresses regret for a lost opportunity to love a stranger.

I must admit I had been secretly harboring a wish (and praying to God) that we would get one of those makeovers for Steve, but I believe that he would get more joy if I could somehow get ABC's Ty Pennington to facilitate Steve in helping someone else.

As a result, I think I'll ask God for an Extreme Soul Makeover, so I can be worthy of my husband.

February 6, 2010

BLESSINGS IN DISGUISE

Thank you for your kind words and encouragement after my last post. I would love to pretend that every day is perfect, but that would not be honest...and one thing that does not belong in healing is dishonesty or avoidance of our reality.

That said, HI EVERYBODY! What a snow event! Last night we went to bed with sideways snow about five inches deep. At 2 a.m. it was swirling with the biggest flakes I've ever seen, about eight inches deep. Then at 3:30 it turned to pelting sleet and rain beating down the snow to about five inches deep again. I noticed all the clocks flashing by 6 a.m., so at some point we lost power, but we awoke to a warm house even so. Thank you, Bob! (Steve's name for God when he was relearning how to speak).

We lost our canopy on the deck—it looks like a dead daddy long-legs, tumbled and crushed by heavy snow and violent wind. We'll have to wait for better weather to dismember it further and cart its carcass away. Several years ago, I would have whined and complained about it, but this whole healing process has really put things into perspective...and a canopy is a THING.

Please do not misunderstand, things are wonderful tools that

CROSSING THE CARING BRIDGE ❦ 129

make life easier, but I used to believe they held more power to make ME more important. I struggled to acquire things, worried about the status of my surroundings and the cut and modernity of my clothing, the trendiness of my home. However, I have since learned that too many things can block the path of a recovering stroke victim, nice clothing is inconvenient when cleaning up spills and shampooing carpet, and too many appliances clutter a countertop when you're trying to organize meds.

When I sit in the chemo-treatment room with Steve and the other patients, my accessories are meaningless, and my handbag is only good for carrying snacks and mints to share. Years ago, I would have pitied someone in my position, but now I see that it has been an amazing gift from Bob (God). As a result, Steve now marvels how so many love him, and his relationship with Bob has deepened immensely. As a result, I have had a whole new world opened to me that I might have missed out on before.

First, I have seen the true hearts and spirits of my colleagues, my neighbors, my family and friends. I have experienced the unconditional kindness of strangers, including a former stranger (now beloved friend) from Iran whose brother is struggling with brain cancer as well. I have seen our children put aside personal agendas to offer selfless service, and neighbors slog through knee-deep snow drifts to deliver a meal. And, I have watched God make good on promises to see us through each day.

Over and over in His Word He reminds us that we are loved and cared for, that our needs will be met. "Consider the birds of the air...neither do they sow or reap or store their grains, but our

Father feeds them. How much more does our Father love you? So, seek first the Kingdom of Heaven and all its righteousness, and these things will be added unto you."

Not until now…not until YOU all, have I truly understood on a visceral level what these words mean. They were something I read or heard read and quoted…nice words…but just words. Now…now that I have had the privilege of this challenge, I see that they are true.

My #1 job is to love and care for my husband and keep the house running efficiently for him. That leaves little time and/or energy for other stuff…that's okay, though, God said not to worry—when we are hungry, you show up with food. When we're frightened, your tender card arrives, your funny or uplifting email comes, or you knock on our door. When we need something, you show up to run errands, to shovel our walk, to pick up downed limbs in our yard, to grab our mail. And, when we've received a bill for insurance, gas, or water, you helped us with generous gifts…many anonymous.

We're humbled, overwhelmed, honored, touched, and blessed by your kindness. We feel loved, encouraged, and cared for, and your prayers truly envelop us and give us comfort. If life had been business as usual, we would have vaguely believed these God promises, but we wouldn't KNOW them in our bones, our hearts, our guts.

My wish is that you trust me on this and that you do not have to face a similar trial, but I can ASSURE you that should your life take a turn, you do NOT have to be afraid. As you have done for us, it will be done for you. The promises are real…and the healing…the healing, I have learned, may or may not come on the physical level, but on the more important level—your heart and soul.

As the author of the book I'm reading right now—*The End of the Spear*—says: "Our bodies are but empty vessels, broken pottery, dried husks that once housed our souls and are shucked off when no longer needed. No disease, no disaster, not deterioration can truly touch that which is eternal."

Thank you, Bob, for the gift of realizing that before it was too late. Bob bless you all, you lovely, lovely angels.

Extra Prayer for Steve

Beloved friends, we had a rough day today. Steve grew weak as the day wore on, his speech became confused, and he had trouble walking or using his right hand/arm. Therefore, I did something I hadn't planned on doing—I opened the disc from the hospital containing Friday's MRI scan and peeked. I wasn't going to do so, because the radiologist's report was not on it; however, I remembered what our recent baseline scan looked like, and I know enough by now to detect major changes.

They were there. While I can't read the fine details, I can see quite a bit of edema or swelling both in the cranium surrounding the brain and in the resected tumor cavity, which has compressed the left hemisphere and caused a midline shift. You GBM tumor friends will understand what that means, and for the rest of us, just know that it isn't optimal. I thought perhaps cabin fever had gotten to Steve, or that he was dehydrated, but his decline throughout the day indicated more.

Therefore, I upped Steve's steroid in the hope of reducing the swelling while I await word from the NO (neuro-oncologist) from Duke. Our Duke appointment was moved from tomorrow to the 18th due to the snow, but I'm hoping for a reading on the scan before then. In any case, I'll keep everyone posted.

A bittersweet update: Our son-in-law Dave will be leaving in a few days, and I must admit that not only will I miss his lovely company, but I'm a little nervous about taking care of things alone if Steve's strength continues to wane. I guess I will just put it in Bob's (God's) ample lap and let Him take care of it as He always does.

I don't know what I would have done these past weeks without Dave, who has literally been a "Bob-send"—so helpful, such good company, and a very hard worker, shoveling us out after two major snowstorms. He has just received news from the Army that he'll be reporting to Valley Forge Military Academy as a gold bar (officer, second lieutenant) recruiter from now until May when he will then report to Ft. Knox for active duty. He has missed spending the last month with our daughter—his new wife—to be here for us—a sacrifice for both.

In the meantime, I request your prayers for both Dave (going to PA) and daughter Chelsea (stationed and finishing school down in TX) that they will safely reunite soon; and please pray for Steve's healing and renewed strength and that my strength will increase as needed. I will need an extra measure to handle whatever comes with even a fraction of the grace shown by so many of my brain-tumor patient/caregiver friends—talk about TOUGH.

Finally, please offer up a prayer of comfort for the G— family. They lost a beloved husband and father today to a GBM brain tumor—brain cancer is claiming our friends at too fast a rate. Thank you all for everything you've done, are doing, and will do. You are truly our lifelines right now.

Bob bless you, jan

Steve and the Unmade Bed

From as far back as I can remember, my mother never left the house until all beds were made. In the beginning, that meant I watched as she first made hers then tidied mine, and later I was shown the proper way to do it and was expected to make my own. She was very precise—sheets pulled tight, blankets smoothed flat, and pillows enfolded just so within the bedspread—one would've thought she'd been in the military. She was even known to have ironed her sheets!

While I didn't pick up all of Mom's cleaning habits, the bed thing stuck. I'm even so neurotic about it that I cannot comfortably get ready or leave home with an unmade bed. For me, it signals the beginning of a new day…the resuming of daily life… that all is well.

Lately, however, the nights have been so disrupted that it's been hard to tell when night ends and day begins. Sometimes we're up so many times that I stagger around like a sleepwalker throughout the day, wondering if anything will ever be normal again. I was in just such a state this morning.

Even though he'd barely slept last night, Steve wanted to be up and dressed at 7 a.m. I went through the routine of getting him ready—toileted, bathed, teeth brushed, shaved, fully dressed, and wheeled to the couch—without much enthusiasm or energy, and I was still in my PJs as I served him his coffee and bran muffin. I knew the nurse was coming to draw Steve's weekly blood sample, so I left Steve with Dave to get myself ready before her arrival.

When I got back to our room, the first thing I saw was the unmade bed. If I were going to skip it any day, today could have easily been justified as that day. I was pressed for time, exhausted, and the fix would've been as simple as closing the bedroom door with no one any the wiser. "Forget it," I told myself, "you don't need to do it today, and besides, you may want to grab a nap in it later." I therefore headed off for the shower.

When I had dried off and dressed, getting ready to hurry back to Steve, I noticed the bed again. In the big scheme of things, it is truly no big deal, but it just seemed wrong to leave it unmade, so I dug in. As I tucked in the sheets and blanket, and as I straightened the comforter and throw pillows, I began to relax. Odd, I thought, to relax while doing a chore, but with each pat and pull I found myself thinking of Steve.

I love this bed, I thought as I walked around to the other side, mainly because Steve had made it in his shop with his strong, loving hands, *and I love this beautiful blanket chest at the foot*. Steve had worked overtime to have them finished quickly for me, and he was so pleased to see how excited I was with them; so, I decided, the very least I can do is honor his effort by making it as neat and comfy as possible, and this meant NOT leaving it torn apart.

I guess that the whole ritual became a metaphor for living with a medical situation. I've heard people say they are "dying of cancer," but I know that Steve only considers himself to be LIVING. He says, "I'm healed while they learn from my body." Therefore, to leave an unmade bed would say that hope is dying, that life is not normal, that there is nothing to expect from this day…and I know differently.

We had a moment today when Steve and I cried together. We held each other, and he told me, very clearly, "You are my best buddy…the love of my life…I don't want us to be apart." I assured him we would be together forever, and he said, "I don't want to lose you or leave you." There was nothing more to say, so we hugged as the tears spilled.

I could feel a flood of tears just waiting to burst forth, but Steve drew himself up and declared, "I am going to get better, and I am going to keep doing that as long as I can." I pulled myself up by my mental bootstraps and smiled. "Sounds great!" And it did.

Suddenly, I was truly glad I'd made the bed…and it did not seem so silly. After all, if Steve is determined to forge ahead against all reasonable odds, then the least I can do is follow his lead. The bed is made…our day has begun…we are getting on with the business of living…and all is well.

Diggin' Out

Rough night last night. Very little sleep—Steve restless and agitated. Today he is very tired and weak, eating little. His balance and endurance were pretty sketchy this morning. He did joke with me a little but fell asleep soon after.

I finally received a call from Duke last night—they agreed with my upping of steroids to reduce his cranial swelling, but they are still waiting for the scans from our local hospital to check tumor activity. Apparently, our scans were sent snail mail instead of FedEx as indicated on the orders…sigh. Duke docs obviously cannot make determinations on anything until they have all the info, so we'll wait.

Steve is not a candidate for hospitalization now as some well-wishers have suggested, because all they can do is what we're already doing at home—plus he's so much more comfortable here. Also, sending the scans over the Internet is not optimal in detecting all the changes, but thanks for all your concerns and suggestions…we appreciate your loving interest. Presently, his vitals are all stable.

Dave is still here and will stay at least until Mac gets down from New York. Mac's tire blew out during the blizzard, so he's trying to fix it in over a foot of snow and ice. His jack broke, so he called for roadside assistance, and when the guy showed up he didn't have a jack on his truck—gotta love the Bronx! Mac's current plans are to be here tomorrow after his first class. Steve told me he was very excited to see him again.

We have chemo tomorrow, and Steve will be even more tired and weak…so I ask you to please keep those prayers going.

These are the difficult times—sometimes I call them the "valley days" (from the 23rd Psalm), and I know there will be more to come. That's okay, because there are so many beautiful moments in between—the mountaintop experiences that leave the valleys in shadow.

Stay warm and dig out safely!

Hi Guys,

We still seem to have more "valley" through which to travel today. Steve was so very weak this morning that he could not stand. I had to bathe him in his wheelchair. He would cry in frustration but whisper "I love you" through each straining moment and gasp "thank you, sweetheart" after each task was finished. I would kiss him each time and tell him not to worry—that's what Valentines do.

We are concentrating on rehydrating him today and we'll stretch him today after chemo if he can tolerate it. We'll also be in contact with Duke about steroid level.

Please offer up your powerful prayers that these steroids do their thing quickly. I also pray that Mac's arrival will make a difference to the good.

Thank you all so much for all you do. I honestly would be lost without each of you. Just knowing you care keeps me from feeling so alone on this journey.

Bob bless you…

Hello Everyone!

Today was angel day! Steve didn't sleep much last night because of post-chemo illness, so we were fading this morning. Steve was out on the couch, so Dave suggested I take a nap. I took him up on it and dropped dead to the world. That's all it took for some excitement to kick up.

For the next hour and a half, Dave played host to quite a few angels, and when I awoke, there were cookies, dinners, candies, and cards. He did his best to get all the names right, so THANK YOU if I miss any of you… What a lovely thing to wake up to, but I'm sorry to miss out on the hugs that always come with the goodies. Bob bless you all for your unfailing, unending kindnesses!!!

Perhaps the most touching of all was from an anonymous angel…let me explain.

Steve is perhaps the most romantic man I know…always looking for an occasion to present me with a gift from his heart. He used to make me things, cut blooms from the roses we planted together, and pick out the perfect card…we never expected or asked each other for expensive things, so the handmade ones were the most precious.

Well, lately, with every Valentine's commercial on TV, Steve would get upset and say he wanted to give me something but wasn't able. He was so worried that I would be disappointed. I must have told him a thousand times that all I wanted was a kiss and to be together.

Today, a florist delivered a dozen red roses with a card from Steve to me. I know he couldn't handle the call or arrange such a thing…and we're being very careful with finances. I read the card and he was confused, because he said he didn't send them, but the card got it exactly right— "You're the love of my life…thank you, Steve."

I assured him that instead of being embarrassed that he didn't send them, he should be pleased that his feelings were obvious to others; therefore, it didn't matter who sent them. Whoever you are…you did a very kind, loving thing…and you clearly know true love when you see it. Thank you for believing in us enough to give such a wonderful gift.

I just hope each of you finds someone to love so much that it's obvious to everyone. So, start by doing what Steve always did when I visited him at work…skip across the parking lot for your hug. That's one of my secret wishes—to have him skip over to me again for his hug.

Note: To this day I still do not know who this angel was, but Bob bless you for this.

The Gift of Loneliness

Today was quiet and sweet. Steve didn't feel up to getting shaved or dressed today, so we stayed in our PJs all day. Dave and Mac were visiting friends, so Steve and I had the house to ourselves—I think that's why Steve was comfortable to do nothing but sleep in my lap. I only got up to bring him meds and food, so no chores got done at all. That's okay as these days do not happen often.

I told him, as I tucked him in a few minutes ago, that tomorrow we shave, dress, and have our therapies. He agreed without complaint. I just hope a full day of sleep will have given him the rest he's needed and that he will awake with more energy and vigor.

Mac and Dave both leave tomorrow, and it will be an adjustment for sure. They're back out this evening, so the house is very quiet again—a preview of what's to come. I guess I will have to acclimate—it's okay though, as the loneliness allows me more time to talk to Bob (Steve's name for God) and to pray for all of you on my list.

We often fight loneliness…or run from it altogether. However, it seems to be that in those dark, empty, and forlorn hours, we can find ourselves drawing closer to our inner selves and to Bob. The outside noise dies down, so we can work on quieting the inner noise. I am as guilty as the next person of fearing these moments…especially when there's been a long period of continuous company and activity, but when I accept the solitude and relax in it, I make peace with it again…and it can almost be my friend.

The pain doesn't dissolve in the quiet, but I can acknowledge it and really feel it, and thereby lessen its bite. By facing it, rather than avoiding or trying to escape it, I can begin to deal with it. It's like lancing a boil…I've never had one, but I've seen it done. Boils are angry, fiery reservoirs of infection under the skin that are painful to the touch, but the only way to heal them is to cut into them, open them up, and drain their poison. It's painful and messy, but it offers relief and healing. Then afterward, you must keep the wound open to the air so it doesn't seal up and fester again.

Pain is, I am finding, a given. If you live, you will have it at some point—trust me on this. The only way to avoid it is to die or curl up in a shell, hidden from the outside world, so you might as well BE dead. Therefore, to avoid pain is to shy away from life. So, I will continue to love my husband—hopefully back to health—but love him despite any pain that it opens me up to, and I will trust that Bob will be with us all the way, because the deeper the solitude, the clearer His voice.

"Be still…and know that I am Bob."

Steve in hospital

Hi everyone,

I am sorry to tell you that we had to take Steve to the ER today where he was diagnosed with blood clots in his right leg. That, of course, explains the severe pain and restlessness he was experiencing over the weekend.

Steve will be in the hospital for several days while they bust the clot. The risk is that clot busters can cause cerebral hemorrhaging, but to ignore such a large number of occlusions would almost assuredly lead to deadly clots to lung or brain. So, weighing the risks with the docs from Duke, we all decided on the blood thinner.

This setback means we cannot travel to Duke for our appointment, but I hope that the scans will make it there, so we can find out how the treatments have been working. Unfortunately, one of the chemo drugs, Av—, is a possible culprit for the clots, so please pray that the cure won't be our undoing.

Thank you, neighbors who brought food and looked after our house; thank you, physical therapist, for suspecting the clot; thank you, ER and medical team at AGH, for a quick diagnosis and consult with Duke and compassionate care; thank you, friends, for bringing me a soda and hugs and encouraging Steve; thank you, Mac, for cleaning the house; and thank you, prayer warriors, for getting down to business.

We love you all, and we can truly feel the love from you. We'll keep you posted.

The Miracle of Morphine

Hi everyone,

Steve is having a better day thanks to the miracle of morphine. If you know Steve well, or have seen him in action, you would know that he avoids pain medicine like the plague. My goodness, the man only took ONE oxycodone after brain surgery and walked out of ICU two days after. The highest he's ever admitted or claimed to be hurting on the one-to-ten pain scale is a four. However, this blood clot (which extends from back of thigh to lower calf) actually received a "four, maybe a five..." on the Steve Calloway pain scale.

We finally convinced him to take a Percocet, which did nothing. Then they shot him up with morphine, which finally took the edge off. According to anyone who's ever had this condition, it's some of the worst pain imaginable...so add that to a brain that is undergoing chemo with a lot of swelling—owww. It breaks my heart to hear him whimper in his sleep...and yes, we're finally having sleep. He is too exhausted to eat or be very conscious because this pain has robbed him of many nights of rest. It's good to finally see him relax, but he cannot afford to lose any more weight.

He will be released in a few days but will receive Lov— injections (blood thinner) twice a day indefinitely. I will be the one who sticks him but finding a little pinch of skin for the needle will be a challenge.

He isn't receiving visitors, because even having the nurses or doctors talk with us in the room hurts him. Please know that he loves you and cherishes your friendship, but he's just not up to any socializing now. We'll keep you updated on when it's okay to come.

My sister-in-law Peggy arrived yesterday and has been a Bobsend. Mac left for school yesterday morning, and he and his sister Chelsea were worried about my being alone. They were so relieved that Peggy came to the rescue, and she was such wonderful support when I decided to have them give Steve morphine—best decision yet (even though he said he wasn't sure he needed it). We have Peggy to thank for getting me home earlier last night for a real meal and sleep. We left a snoring Steve, so it wasn't complete torture for me.

Upon arriving at AGH this morning, the nurses were pleased to inform us that he'd slept well all night. However, when I opened his door, he was in the process of crying and calling out for me. Big tears rolled down his cheeks when he saw me, and he sobbed in my arms like a child. "They took you away and I was calling and calling for you, but they wouldn't answer me, and I was yelling and everything…" He caught his breath between sobs and heaved and hiccupped like a toddler waking up after a nightmare.

It really brought home the fact that he's as innocent and vulnerable as a child, and that being with him is being on HOLY GROUND…a great and sacred responsibility. Even Mac, the other night, very seriously told me, "Steve needs you, Mom, and I think you need to always be with him. He asks for you all the time like when you leave to take a shower…he gets panicky if you're not right there. Don't worry though…you take care of him now, and I'll take care of you guys when I graduate." Pretty compassionate for a 21-year-old, but something I will never saddle him with.

So, that is our update. Duke is still awaiting scans. I faxed them the written radiology report, and I ordered the scans sent from AGH for the THIRD time. I even offered to pay for them myself. A GBM caregiver friend told me she mails the scans to Duke herself to avoid these things, so next time that's what I'll do. Sigh…we are in limbo not knowing how the treatment is progressing and what exactly is happening in Steve's brain.

Some well-meaning folks have grilled me on the scans as if I have control over them. I've done my best to get them to Duke, and I assure you, friends, that no one wants the results more than I. I even stood over the secretary in charge of sending them with a doctor by my side while I reordered them FedExed…again. Pray they make it soon!

Thank you so much for the delightful and delicious meals and treats. I barely have energy to make my bed, let alone cook, so they are deeply, deeply appreciated. And, as always, thank you so very much for your thoughts and prayers. We have truly felt them during this last setback, and with them, we will emerge from the valley once again. Prayers and morphine—a beautiful combination… Now, if they'll just give me a little…

Love y'all…

Hi Everyone,

Update as of noon is that the clot is breaking up with Lov—. Steve still has pain—just less. I'm told I will have to give blood thinner by injections twice per day indefinitely. I can handle that.

Steve is too weak to get himself into chair or stand, so we cannot go home until our Hoyer lifting equipment arrives tomorrow. Without such devices in place, they were going to insist I send him to a rehab hospital or nursing home—I cannot do that. I know he desperately doesn't want such a thing, so I must have a plan in place for how to bring him home. I'm told they will send him by ambulance squad, so get ready, Ocean Pines FD!

Unfortunately, Steve has been aspirating what little food he has tried to eat, so I asked them to bring him a soft diet. He did much better with the pudding and yogurt, so I'll have to put my blender back into service tomorrow.

YAY! Duke finally has our scans, but our neuro-oncology doc is with patients until later today. Hope to hear from her by end of day. We are especially interested in knowing the results as they will dictate how we proceed from here—good or bad. I pray for good results as well as strength to face what's next. Whatever happens, I have promised Steve that I will be with him every step of the way…no matter what.

To those of you who recently sent goodies—Laura and John B., Kaye Y., Jane D., Dollie G., Karen S., Diane G., and Kathleen

O.—THANK YOU!!! I don't know when I'll get back to my thank-you note writing, but I wanted you to know how very sweet you are and appreciative we are. Jack and Betty A.—Steve and I LOVE the photo!!!! It brings us such joy! Rev. Lindsay and Rev. Rick—thanks for the blessing and ashes anointing. Jim and Nancy H., thanks for running interference at home and receiving deliveries; we so appreciate your love and prayers.

I will update you all as soon as I know anything further. Thank you for being so wonderful.

*A note from the present looking back. Our neuro-oncologist called me later that evening to discuss the scans that she had just received. She confirmed what I already knew in my head but didn't want to let into my heart. Steve's cranium was once again full of tumor despite the new treatment.

"We could try something else..." she said, her voice trailing off.

"Dr. D, I feel him slipping away," I whispered. "He only stirs to reach for me. He's not eating or drinking or speaking anymore."

"Jan, he has fought a good fight, honey, but his brain is so tired... I think it is time to let him...rest." She patiently waited for me to process, but she had spoken what I already knew.

"I want to bring him home now." My voice quavered. "I want him home with me until..." Then tears streamed down my face as I gave into the sobs I'd held back for so long. When I paused to catch my breath, I was strangely comforted to hear her crying too. We wept together a little longer, then both sighed deeply at the same time, collecting ourselves for the last tasks before us.

"I think it's time to authorize hospice, Jan, so I will make the call to the hospitalist for you now. Is that okay?"

I agreed, and there, in that little impersonal phone room next to the hospital chapel, I quietly opened the door to allow Death to make his OFFICIAL sanctioned entry.

Hi Friends and Family. This isn't an easy one to write.

We brought Steve home by ambulance and he is resting in his hospital bed. He is surrounded by his family, and he is comfortable. He sleeps all the time now, but we know he is peaceful. We respectfully ask that you do not visit at this time. We ask for your continued prayers for courage and strength. I will offer more later, but for now I would like to return to his side. Thank you and Bob bless you.

*Additional note written at present looking back.

When we were unloading Steve from the ambulance to bring him into the house, he roused enough to look around, realizing he was home and not at the medical center or at Duke. He then asked incredulously—speaking for the first time in days— "So this is it?" I remember it as if it just happened.

Our boys from Ocean Pines, Larry and Glenn, the young paramedics Steve had mentored who were like sons to us, insisted on being the crew to bring our Steve home for what we knew would be the last time. I would have had it no other way. We all stood frozen for a moment, not knowing how to answer, but on some level, Steve must have put it together that there were going to be no more treatments, no more surgeries, no more visits to the hospitals…and it's as if he resigned himself to the truth that he had come home to die.

He sighed and laid his head on the pillow, falling back into a deep unconsciousness. Somehow, in that moment, I felt as if I had betrayed him, lied to him, misled him, let him down. As if I was responsible for letting Death into the house for good.

I cannot ever remember feeling so utterly wretched as I did at that moment, and I vowed to make his remaining time as easy and sweet as possible.

Hospice arrived, patiently, lovingly, and graciously explaining to me the physical process of dying. The chaplain sat quietly while the nurse walked me through each step, gently laying out expectations. I knew it was coming. I could feel Death at the table with us, imagining him nodding in solemn agreement with her description.

Strangely, knowing how Death tended to work in such a case as this was helpful, even comforting. It took the mystery out of it and made Death almost familiar to me. I listened, half picturing each stage we were facing yet somehow thinking we might just somehow be different.

I prepared the area where we would care for Steve with supplies, moved an air mattress into the dining room where we'd assembled the hospital bed so that I could remain next to him always. I had been shown how to administer the palliative medications and how to care for his basic physical needs, thinking I would be all organized when he awoke…but I was never to truly hear his voice again…he never fully awakened after that, but he knew I was there…and I knew he knew.

February 22, 2010

The Sacred Journey

I write this as I sit at the side of my husband. I can barely take my hand away from his long enough to type, and I stop continuously to pat him, kiss him, and listen to his breath…making sure the next one follows. His body is fading…his breath faltering… and flesh diminishing…yet his soul is expanding. He has practically become spirit stuff…radiant light…emanating such a love that embraces all who bend to kiss his now tiny hands or caress his weary brow.

When I bend my lips to his ear to assure him how much he is loved, his cracked and dried lips mouth it back. When I tell him that we will always be together, his eyelids flutter. I must be careful though that the ferocity of my love for him does not become a tight bond that tethers him to his worn-out vessel, so I assure him that bodies do not matter…that love can survive the passing of the clay.

I remind him that our souls have melded long ago and that he will be my companion every moment of each day…that he can guide me in caring for his roses, rejoice in the happiness of our children, and soothe my heart in the lonely night. I told him he can even go to work with me someday.

Some of you may feel anger or sadness that our time together was relatively brief—thinking it unfair or that God is cruel; but let me assure you that Steve loved me with such an unconditional, unbounded love that it will surely last me the rest of my life. The passing of his earthly housing will not diminish its power. He would always say, "I've searched for you all of my lives…and I'm not about to leave you now." I think he finally realizes that he's not remaining in quite the manner he'd expected, but he will remain just the same. I do think he knows that now.

So, Steve has one foot in our world and one foot in the spiritual. He is listening to the sighs of his family here, while at the same time hearing the calls of loved ones who've already passed over. I believe he is reaching the end of his journey, where he will stand before the throne of Grace and hear the words we all know are due him— "Well done, good and faithful servant…I have prepared a place for you in my Father's house… Welcome home."

There will be tears here on earth, but when we get alone in our quiet place, we will hear a great rejoicing of angels who now have Steve—shining, loving, laughing, tender, generous, forgiving Steve—to make the streets of gold even brighter with his smile. But I also know that he will remain here in the hearts and minds of all who love him well. And when you think your heart cannot go on for grief…he will call your attention to a beautiful sunset, a blooming rose, a strutting bird, a busy squirrel, a twinkling star, and you will know that Steve is watching you, while he hangs out on a heavenly park bench with his "bestest buddy," Bob.

I am heartbroken to tell you that my beloved Steve passed away in my arms this morning. I know his body is finally at rest and that the dark will not be so dark now that a new angel is there to watch over us. I am just wondering now if it will ever NOT hurt to breathe.

I was blessed to be surrounded with loving family, and hospice was a Bob-send. Arrangements for Steve's memorial service will be announced soon.

Thank you all for your kindnesses and prayers. Please pray for all the other GBM families who are struggling and suffering and pray that life will feel worth living again. That's what my love would want.

"Death ends a life, not a relationship." —Mitch Albom

February 27, 2010

Dear Friends and Family,

The memorial service celebrating Steve's life will take place on Saturday, March 6th, 2010 at 2 p.m. at the Ocean Pines Volunteer Fire Department—911 Ocean Parkway, Ocean Pines, MD.

In lieu of flowers, contributions can be made in honor of Steve to either OPVFD at the above address, or to Coastal Hospice, Inc., 2604 Old Ocean City Rd. Salisbury, MD 21801.

Thank you and Bob bless you all.

Farewell, Jack Calloway

Steve has been busy lately. He was reconnecting with all his loved ones who've passed over, and today, just two days after being in Heaven, he brought his father home. "Dad" Jack Calloway, my beloved father-in-law, passed away today in Salisbury. He was a lovely man who left his sense of humor all over Steve. We will miss him so much.

Please pray for strength to send them both off well.

The Beginnings of Grief…

I wish I had some wonderful incident to impart, but I think I'll just update you on how things stand.

I kissed my love's body good-bye for the last time today. I insisted on being the last person to touch him before his cremation, and the funeral home generously obliged.

After Steve passed, but before they picked him up on Friday, I bathed his body with rosewater in memory of his love for roses. It was an honor to prepare my love's body. I tried to show him with each movement how much I love him, and I prayed that his soul was free to watch without pain or sorrow.

I must admit that I was hoping and expecting Steve to show his soul to me right away…give me a sign…talk to me…touch me…but I guess he was busy preparing to bring his dad home too. My father-in-law died two days later, on Sunday.

I try not to be selfish, begging God to let me keep Steve all for myself, but I imagine Steve's had his hands full. I keep thinking that he is waiting for quiet time…I've been surrounded by people 24/7 without break. Steve always loved for us to be alone together, and that is what I'm craving too. He would often say…"I just want to be with you…just us." I suspect that hasn't changed.

So, I will struggle to hold myself together for Dad's funeral and through Steve's memorial, then I will closet myself up in desperate hope that I will see my love again. Breathing hurts and does not come without sobs and gasps. No thing or no one can ease the pain of life without Steve. Nothing seems important now, and I only press on for the sake of my children.

So, be patient with me if I take a bit longer to answer your questions…if I don't jump at your kind offers…don't be offended if I don't take your calls or answer the door. I am grieving a love that very few have ever experienced. My heart is torn asunder, and only God can carry me now.

There never has been anyone like Steve…he was one in a million, and I was the luckiest woman on earth to be so loved by him. I will try to hold on to that.

Thank you for your prayers.

Dad Jack's Final Call

Steve's dad, Jack Calloway, would have been proud of his FINAL CALL today—the term they use for a fireman's funeral. The tear-stained faces of his dwindling generation standing side by side with eager young men brand-new to the department lined the aisles. They took turns standing watch over the coffin of this 59-year veteran of Mardela Springs, MD Fire Dept. Jack was well-guarded before his last ride, while young and old paid their last respects.

After the service, tough hands in white gloves tenderly lifted his casket onto the waiting engine for his final ride—the line of mourners stretching far behind. The engine, festooned with mourning cloth, led a reverent procession over country roads, down the highway, and through town. All along the way, firefighters, troopers, and respectful bystanders stood at attention and saluted. Townsfolk lined the streets the final block past the firehouse, and the whistle blew for Dad Jack's last call.

The sun was shining, the birds were singing, and the wind rustled through the trees. It was a glorious moment in a wonderful life, and Jack would have been proud...I know I was.

We love you, Dad, and will miss you more than you know... but look who's waiting for you on the other side.

Some folks often feel a lack of closure when there is no body for viewing. Steve's wishes were for cremation, so I searched for just the right photo that captured his loving spirit, but none was just right. Then, I lost my mind and decided to do his portrait today in pastels and ink. It was taken from a pic on my phone at the very moment he heard he was cancer free (in 08). I felt him over my shoulder the whole night while I worked, and I was pleased when it was done. It is how I will forever hold him in my heart and mind. This is my love.

Additional note:

The funeral itself was a deeply moving affair. Hundreds upon hundreds of people attended, traffic was diverted by police, and arches were created over the roads by ladder trucks from multiple fire companies. MD State Senator Jim Mathias delivered the eulogy; the fire chief officiated; Steve's lifelong friend and firefighting buddy, Phil, gave a tribute; and a fellow paramedic and longtime friend, Harvey, read a poem, after which scores of uniformed firefighters from all over the state stepped up to the urn and portrait, one by one, and crisply saluted, some with stoic dignity, while others fought the tears that tracked down their well-worn faces. All the while, the haunting and beautiful bagpipes played, marking the existence of a man who had saved countless lives and limbs, who had delivered babies, who had comforted the dying, encouraged those who could still make it to hang with him, who had taught thousands to be better medics and first responders, and a man who had sowed seeds of love and laughter all along the journey.

As "Amazing Grace" came to a close, the memorial flag was folded and gently handed to me, and I faced a waiting gauntlet of saluting heroes—a phalanx of young and old, men and women who had shared that life of balancing both danger and long hours of tedium, wearing uniforms and badges of different companies, but who were all united that day by their love for a man who always took the time to smile and be genuinely kind.

So, flanked by our brothers and sisters, we solemnly carried his ashes from the funeral to the hall where we would join in celebration. Strange, but there was a palpable void when Steve Calloway's remains passed, fillable only by love that we now had to share with one another.

The truth about grieving…stage one.

Hi Everyone, I haven't been able to write for a while because I'm learning about grief. I thought I knew what grief looked and felt like after my father's and mother-in-law's deaths, but truly NOTHING could've prepared me for this.

With a house full of family all pulling together to take care of Steve in his final days, there wasn't much time or opportunity for grief to rush in. It could only seep in around the edges, winding its way into my heart. Tears were present but checked in the effort of hospice care and final arrangements.

It wasn't until after Dad Jack's funeral and Steve's memorial on Saturday that I found myself in an empty, quiet house. Gone were the dignified ceremonies, haunting bagpipes, impressive processions with their comforting traditions and heartfelt salutes. Gone were the people rushing around to ensure I had a drink, a tissue, a chair, some food, a hug…

Solitude finally! I had thought fleetingly…I had almost even embraced the prospect of loneliness in the hope of getting a sign, message, or SOMETHING from Steve. That expectation was short-lived, however, as the enormity of my loss hit me with tsunami force. So, after a fretful night, I vowed to flee the house this morning.

I went over to the firehouse to a loving welcome but realized that my husband would never skip out to my car to kiss me again. I went to the bank but realized I would be the only one on the account from now on. Finally, I went to the grocery store and promptly forgot how to shop for just myself.

It was the first time in many months that I didn't have a list of special foods, dietary supplements, or high-calorie treats for Steve. Also missing was the list of kid foods to feed that gang at home and goodies for sharing during a movie we all finally agreed upon. No, this shop was only for me...and I didn't know what to do.

My grief has robbed me of an appetite, and every label seemed written in a foreign language and each box almost too heavy to lift. I grabbed a few essentials to sustain life when it hit me that grief slices life down to bare, raw survivorship.

Grief and pain—I'm told, and I've said—are necessary for healing, but I can tell you they are completely disregarding of your plans. Grief's waves can rush in with regular force, requiring you to time your hopping and ducking to avoid drowning...and grief can also slam you from nowhere like a rogue wave that will capsize you in an unsuspecting instant. When it does, the results are violent, messy, leaving detritus in its wake.

At those times, you are sure your death is imminent...your heart pounds, adrenaline courses through your veins, your head swims, and panic engulfs you. You know you cannot possibly survive the onslaught, and you secretly wish you won't.

That's the best way I know to tell you how I'm feeling and to introduce...or reintroduce you to grief and the pain it drags with it.

How could Charlie Brown ever have called it "good"?

Be Still and Know That I Am Bob...or Steve (Grief second stage)

I don't know how many more signs Bob (God) and Steve need to give me. People I run into, notes I've received, daily devotionals...all tell me to be patient and listen...that I've put the request out there and now it's time to wait. So, this is what came to me first...

A picture/mini-vision just popped into my mind of a person scouring the ground for loose change. Head is down, hunched over, brow furrowed in intense concentration, while feverishly pacing and retracing steps. Frustration oozes from his pores and sighs of disgust burst forth unchecked. Finally, after hours and days of fruitless searching, he throws his hands up in surrender and despair and cries, "Where lies all this change I've been hearing about? All these pennies?!" He freezes...eyes now wide open to match his gaping mouth.

There before him is an outstretched palm holding a one-hundred-dollar bill, and a still, small voice says, "It's been here all the time... you just needed to look up."

This is where I am. I am reminding myself to look up, relax, and know that Bob and Steve have been waiting for me to slow down, stop muttering, give up fretting, and just look up.

Please pray for me to learn to hold up, shut up, and look up.

Bless you. Janni

March 11, 2010

Roller Coaster of Grief (stage three)

Today began with a phone call from a beloved childhood friend who sent her warm hugs by cell, so I smiled and made my bed. Then calls from my kids and sister made me grin…and I did a load of laundry. Next, I decided to try to eat some cereal, and I saw the box of pecan twirls that Steve so loved…and I broke down in heaving sobs.

I showered off the salt and let the water pummel my head while I sang one of my favorite old hymns, "Precious Lord Take My Hand." I threw on some clothes, fed Chelsea's puppy, and ate that bowl of cereal…still humming. I checked my email and read about a friend whose husband is in the fight of his life, and the agony of young husbands with brain tumors flooded back. I prayed for his well-being and her peace and went on to my next email. It was a loving, soothing letter from a cherished friend about messages from the afterlife. I sighed, wishing the house was not so quiet.

Just then, a knock on the door brought another friend and a hug and some wise, helpful advice about living…and I found myself laughing. Laughing…isn't that forbidden? I'm a widow, a husk, a wearer of black, married only to God and grief now… right?

I shook off the thought and went to get my hair cut. I made it as far as the center and decided to go to my favorite clothing shop first for a look around. I selected a few things, headed to the dressing room, and put on my first item. I looked in the mirror and wondered who the tired, gray-headed, sad woman was staring at me. The dress was cute…but all I could think was there was no one…no Steve…to say, "Oh honey, that's so pretty on you!"— even if it was said from love, not reality. I gasped, got dressed quickly, and bolted from the store before the sobs broke loose.

Haircut forgotten, I must have been a sight on the drive home, and by the time I'd made it home, my phone was ringing… It was daughter Chelsea, calling to check on me. She knew immediately that I'd been crying, and I related my dressing room scene. She said, "That's right, Mom, he wasn't outside waiting for you to model; he can get IN the dressing room now, and he's pretty happy about that!" So, I laughed again.

Up and down, laughter and tears, guilt and smiles, joy and pain… The Roller Coaster of Grief—it's a wild ride and sometimes I want to throw up. I just look forward to the moment I can let go, even enjoy the weightless thrill, knowing I'll find my way back to the station…windblown, heart pounding, but intact.

First, let me extend love and condolences to a new angel, firefighter Charlie V, who surrendered his valiant fight to a brain tumor. He has joined Steve, and I imagine they're already talking about fire engines they've loved. Please pray for his wife, Cindy, and their family. They need God's special comfort.

Baby Steps (Grief stage four...you DO know I'm making up these stages as I go, right?)

Today was...well...roller-coaster weird again. I started out the morning with Chelsea's puppy snuggled so tightly that when I awoke, I thought this was all just a bad dream and that my man was curled behind me. The laugh was on me though when the little mutt started gnawing on my arm in play. As I was rubbing the sleep from my eyes, the phone rang, and the day brightened with tender, kind words of love and support from a treasured friend.

The better part of the day was dedicated to the business of "living after dying"—insurance, legal stuff, banking, etc.—just what you want to do amidst the grief. I realized that this was probably NOT the time to be taking care of financial matters as I could barely remember my own name, but alas, time was of the essence.

On my travels, as the day grew dreary with fog and I wondered how I would slog through it, I ran into another angel who gave me a hug filled with such warmth and love that I barely noticed the pouring rain. How does God know just when to send these people??? Oh right...He's God.

Calls from fam and friends continued, and I was urged by the younger set to think about coloring my gray hair and freshening my cut. I had been buzzing my hair off for over two years in support of Steve's chemo head. My cut had seen many better days… so early this evening I went to a big girl salon and told them to do what they wanted. Someone at the front desk knew I was recently widowed, and therefore everyone was "extra nice" to me. I appreciated it, though, because I ended up with a sassy cut and a color I could never have managed by myself from a box. (Thank you, angels who treated me to that pamper session.)

Funny but supportive texts flew in, and I was able to express my nervousness while being reminded that coloring my hair wasn't at all a slight to my husband's memory—I struggle with survivor's guilt…A LOT. A recently widowed friend put it so eloquently: We have it extra hard because we lost our husbands through LOVE, not divorce or hatred. Therefore, the business of living can seem insensitive; but if they were alive, we'd all still be together. Separation IS NOT A CHOICE in this case.

So, I have a fun new cut and color…while I sit at home channel surfing on a Friday night. That's funny when you think about it. Sigh…well, at least the puppy has something new to look at while eating her kibble.

The Sun Will Come Out…Tomorrow? (Grief stage 5, but who's keeping track?)

God is good. The rain fell in torrents, water ran in rivulets, and fog poured forth like…um…dried ice? How cliché of me.

Anyway, I heard all of you…and I mean ALL OF YOU who helped me see the futility of guilt over being alive when my beloved Steve is not. You reminded me that he loved life and fun, and you reminded me that he wants me to do the same. While I'm not singin' in the rain yet, or romping in puddles, I DID go get a new sun hat at the outlet mall. You see…the sun WILL come out again, and I want to be ready. Thanks, Gina, for being my chauffeur and cheering section today!

Keep praying…I'm such a work in progress.

And…just when you're ready for sun….

http://www.youtube.com/watch?v=-3KQTOAtVcw

Toby Keith's "Cryin For Me"—have your tissues handy—sigh…

Additional note: while editing this and re-reading it, I clicked on the link to see if the song was still there and it was. I shed a few tears in remembrance, then noticed that YouTube had made another suggestion related to my original selection. The song was called "With You" from the soundtrack of the Broadway hit musical Ghost. *Curious, I opened and listened and found it just as, if not MORE, impactful— "hauntingly beautiful." I urge you to listen for yourself as a good cry is purgative.*

March 15, 2010

Sucker punch (grief stage 6...I think)

Today was hard...flat-out rough. If it weren't for my sister, Peggy, who took the wheel, my ship would have grounded and broken up in the surf. She was an angel who swooped in and recognized my need. She found me immobilized by the most common of things. I wanted to pay my bills, change my bedsheets, do the laundry, clean out my fridge, and vacuum, but I was paralyzed. I would head to one chore and be immediately pulled to another, incapable of finishing one.

Peggy guided me to the sofa, made me some tea and toast, and helped me concentrate on the finances by doing everything else. I dug in and was making decent progress when it came time for the financial phone calls that every widow dreads...the ones where you must report your loss. I held it together just fine until I was asked, "Was the death natural?"

Natural? Natural! A massive brain tumor in a young vibrant, lovely man...natural? NO! I wanted to scream...NO! There is NOTHING natural about losing your husband so young!!! Of watching him die in your arms!!! My breath caught, my voice shook, and I explained. Somehow, the compassionate representative on the line got me through, and it was on to the next. Each call brought the same question, and though I'd heard it, I choked up every time.

That's the weird thing about grief. It's so darned sneaky. I can buy a hat one moment, laugh at the puppy's antics with my sister the next, and be blindsided by something innocuous like filling out my census form. I answered the questions, through my tears, and realized how lonely writing "one occupant" can be.

I fully realize that there are thousands of people who've faced this and worse and survived. I know that time will help me adjust…time and the love of dear, sweet friends…I know all of this. But right at this moment, it is happening to me. It's my season of sorrow, and I am feeling it—like a sucker punch. At this point, I'm doubled over, with the breath knocked out of me, unable to speak, wondering if I'm going to collapse. Having taught karate, I know this feeling well…and I know that if you hold still and wait, your core relaxes enough to allow that first gasp. Then slowly, with discomfort, your lungs will fill, the pain will begin to subside, and you'll be able to stand.

With a little time, the effects of the sucker punch go away, but you will now guard yourself a little more from life's onslaughts… and you will know how it feels for the next victim. You can't always prevent them, but I think you can survive them… You're never sure, though, until you, yourself, actually do.

Spring Always Comes—grief stage 7

Whether we're ready or not… spring always comes with the first blooms. They are the earth's first blush when the matriarch of winter isn't looking. Today our first bloom opened. It is one of the ones I planted this fall for us to enjoy this spring. This fall, Steve had slowed down, and I knew something wasn't right, but there was no overt sign of his cancer returning; however, something deep in my being (God or gut) told me, "Plant hundreds of bulbs…don't ask…just do it." So, I did.

I remember Steve's enthusiasm as I showed him what would be popping up at different times. Some would be stunning in color, some delicate, some warmly familiar, and one would even look as if plucked from the fertile mind of Dr. Seuss! It took me hours to plant them all and many MORE hours to undo my cramping back, but by the end of a day, there were buried treasures all over the yard.

I decided not to map them out…I wanted us to forget where they were and be delightfully surprised with each new shoot, each new bud, each new explosion of life. Forget them I did, and they were the last things on my mind when we discovered the new tumor. Winter took over, figuratively and literally. God buried us in snow as Death buried us in grief. Shades were drawn at home, and clouds put out the sun. The cold wind froze the tears on my face, and I was sure there would never be another spring.

I guess I was wrong…something that happens a lot. You see, while the bulbs slept, drawing strength from the soil, all I could envision was everlasting winter. The world without Steve in it seemed a frozen, barren wasteland, devoid of any life. I think that happens a lot in winter—the season of rest and solitude. The leaves drop, removing all pleasant distraction, and we're forced to contemplate the bare branches of our souls. Then, just as we accept this solitude as the new norm, a tiny green shoot captures our attention, and we marvel at it as if for the first time ever.

As I watched my love dying, the shoots were growing, and I was indignant at their indifference. They were mocking me…my silly plans for life and happiness…reminding me of my insignificance. As I came and went from home to attend to the business of after-death, I would ignore them, avoid them, and look away. But today…today…I forgot myself for just a moment and glanced down to find my first bloom.

It was only a daffodil—the commonest of bulbs, the cliché of spring—but it stopped me short. "It's okay," it seemed to whisper, "I'm not here to hurt you… I'm here to remind you that beauty, life, and happiness never left. They just lay dormant, respectfully waiting until you were ready." Suddenly, I was filled with warmth and a tender blush of love. I had planted these treasures with love for my husband, with love for beauty, and I trusted them to grow with only God's help.

I had put them there... I was responsible. And then it hit me. Perhaps the still, small voice that told me to do it was God. Perhaps He knew that my winter would be bleak and life a frozen pond. Perhaps He knew that Steve's love for flowers would inspire me to invest in a future not yet seen. By planting these bulbs, I did invest in the future...in the prospect of spring. I had no idea what would happen, but I prepared for it to be lovely. I believed in spring long before it was due...and despite my anguish, tears, and bereavement, it still arrived for me.

In a single bloom, Steve and Bob showed me that life continues, that beauty transcends sorrow, and that love invested yesterday will always brighten your tomorrow. I think Steve, in his relaxed, comfortable, and deeply loving way, just gave me my first big sign. He reminded me that spring always comes.

March 19, 2010

Hello Beloved Friends and Family.

My wish for you is that you are living each day with passion, loving each other with abandon, and thanking Heavenly Father with all your heart for His generous blessings.

Steve's legacy of love and encouragement is living on, and dear friends have begun a scholarship fund to assist young high school men and women whose passion lies in emergency medical response.

Members of OPVFD are sponsoring the following event to raise money to invest in tomorrow's "Steves." I can think of no greater tribute to a man who believed in passing it on and paying it forward.

So, please join me for the 1st Annual STEVE CALLOWAY Memorial Scholarship Pancake Breakfast, $6 per person, Saturday, May 29th, 2010, 7:30 to 11 at the Ocean Pines Community Center. Tickets may be purchased in advance or at the door. For tickets and info please call: Ocean Pines Fire Dept @ 410-641-8272

Thank you all, and I hope to see you there. God bless you, jan

Journal Final Comments: I think it fitting to end my journal here with two of the many things Steve loved: good home cooking and investing in the lives of young people. Pancakes and dreams…a perfect way to keep Steve Calloway's memory going. Thank you, Ocean Pines Fire Department, for making it happen. God bless you and keep you safe as you do the same for others.

Part III

The Aftermath—
Death Takes His Leave

So, Death came for Mr. Stephen Calloway after all. It wasn't as simple as I think he had originally thought, but in the end, Death always leaves with his prize. The thing is, that by the time he had taken Steve, Death and I had made peace. The textbooks call it anticipatory grieving where one has time to prepare and compared to someone whose loved one was taken suddenly and without warning—it is a little easier to know Death is coming; however, it is no less painful. In fact, watching someone virile fade away and lose his grasp on this world is crushingly hurtful. Either way these truths remain: Death hurts as much when he takes his time as when he doesn't, and the only way we can ever prepare is to know that no matter what—he IS going to come.

I look back on my journal, which took me great courage to reread and thus "relive," and I see a person evolving through the visit from Death. Reading it, knowing the outcome, I can see myself as sweetly naive at times, full of almost silly optimism and blind faith, but I sometimes miss and admire that woman more than I am comfortable admitting. I sometimes think I was a better person then…more grounded…and I wonder what happened to the woman who faced Death and kept on smiling and encouraging others. Especially when little, silly, mundane things threaten to stir me up today.

It is important to remember, however, that tougher times call for and bring out a tougher person. It is rather like a warrior trained for battle. He or she clads himself in armor, straps on a weapon, and charges into battle valiantly, knowing that the enemy is at hand. It is second nature because it is life and death and we know the import of the action. Yet, that same soldier, after the battle, very often collapses with exhaustion, is rattled by noises, bolts awake to phantom intruders in the middle of the night and struggles to cope with even the simplest of daily activities. Hyper-vigilance of a face-to-face with Death can do that at first—allow us to dig deep and rise to levels of courage and strength that we never dreamed possible and to find beauty in the tiniest, most insignificant of kindnesses. Then, when he retreats, we collapse, paralyzed by the most insignificant of chores or challenges.

Guard down, we're softer, more vulnerable, more human, and more real. Being alive is a constant dance between the two extremes because Death is a daily occurrence, sometimes near or sometimes quite distant, but always present. Therefore, rather than fear Death, perhaps we can see him for the transformer that he is. He is, as I said before, the great equalizer, the great humbler, the great kindness-motivator, the great introspection-stimulator, the great compassion-promoter, and the great reminder for us to see today as a gift—THE PRESENT.

Death takes things from us, but also opens and clears new paths we would have never considered as well. He can inspire us to greater service for a cause that is bigger than ourselves. He can force us to finally choose a road we've never traveled or try an activity that we wouldn't have considered or have been able to consider before. Death can soften our hearts toward others' suffering and make us realize the futility of judging others, and he can bring us closer to those still living—especially our own selves. Most of all, however, Death can drive us, coax us, lure us, or gently lead us into the loving, open arms of our Creator, our Father, who wants nothing more than to pull us into His spiritual lap and stroke our hair, telling us everything will be all right.

I could easily end this book right here…making a case that a death can lead to beauty, but I have a sense that more needs to be said. Death is also very personal. There is no statute of limitations on grieving, but when it blocks one's ability to move on in life, then that can be a problem. Although Death may interrupt our present joy, Death NEVER intends to prohibit us from future joy or peace or comfort.

As a young widow, I had a lot of loving support, but sadly, I also had a lot of folks who had opinions about how I should conduct my grieving. What few people considered was that I had lived with the specter of Death in my living room for close to three years before my husband physically died, and although I hoped and prayed like crazy for a miracle, he died nonetheless.

The miracle happened, but not the way we had planned. Through Steve's death, thousands were touched by his story and his life in some way, and much beauty survived and bloomed as a result. People were kinder to each other, marriages grew stronger, families closer, and everyone grew more grateful for the simple gift of everyday living. I certainly found transformation in it, yet all along, because I was with Steve 24/7, I could see a steady decline, and God was gently allowing me to know that Death was going to collect—a truth I mostly hid from the readers of my blog for fear that they would lose hope.

Hence, I would secretly cry in the wee hours of the night for what I privately knew was coming…so much so that Mr. Death and I were able to share the same space at the end, and I was able to kiss my husband good-bye and allow him to go.

Although my peace with this was deep, it didn't make it hurt any less, but I knew Steve wanted me to live on. After I was able to be alone and quiet, I received all kinds of messages from him that we had planned, and one day, he blessed my new beginning with an unmistakable sign that had been foretold by a godly woman in a dream, and there were important people in my life present to witness it. Steve was happy "up there with Bob" and all who'd gone before, and wanted me to be happy too—so why was it so hard for everyone around me to accept that?

I can only say what I know…and that is that everyone experiences life and death through his or her personal filter, and to impose that filter on another is naive at best and cruel at worst. After three years of bitter heartbreak veiled in smiles and hope, I had had my share of sorrow and I was ready for a little joy. What earthly good could I possibly bring the world as a ghastly gray, hand-wringing, sobbing, mourning widow who pulls her blinds and withers away?

But the world who had come to my aid, rallied around me, and loved me through the death was forcing my hand in making a choice. There were many who wanted nothing but joy for me, while there were others who had become quite comfortable with the wise widow…always home…always so easy to pity… ready to pray for them, but also so easy to dismiss. Death didn't just take Steve Calloway, Death shook up the whole household, forcing us to reexamine our values, our thoughts, our aspirations, our flaws, and leaving us with a choice. A choice to crumble and curse him as he ruined our lives and stole our future, or to wave him good-bye, humbler, wiser, clearer, and filled with courage to live another day.

So, I shook off the dust of others' opinions of how a widow should die to happiness, and I stepped forward into the light of a new day—a little wobbly but determined to make joy from ashes because of one glorious man's incredible encounter with Death.

The Walking Dead

A lot of tears were shed revisiting this encounter with Death, and during this writing I often felt a deep sadness not only for the obvious loss of Steve, but for all the other relationships that have suffered along the way—loss of more family and friends, dissolution of other marriages, divergent paths of growing kids who seek new futures farther away, and relocation from old friends and familiar places to name a few. These were clearly offset by the abundant outpouring of love from above and all around, but I felt it was okay to examine the sadness, and I have never lost sight of the great healing that has resulted from this experience (which I think I described throughout the journal).

Bob (God) continued and continues to bless me to this day, even though not all paths have been smooth and all roads straight. He never promised that they would be, but He did promise to accompany us all along the journey and deliver us to new destinations by our sides. Bob is always at work for our good—sometimes behind the scenes, however—and sometimes it is only later that we discover how. One thing I can say is that is it simply easier to trust Him than question Him. Case in point:

As I was writing the opening of the book after having reassembled the journal, reading and correcting typos through the blur of tears, I went in for a long overdue mammogram. I used to be religious about getting them annually as my mother and grandmother each had breast cancer, so I was shocked I had let six years pass since my last one (I know, I know—I'm a nurse for Heaven's sake). I was deep into my work when I received a call from the doctor requesting that I have additional testing. This was a new doctor for me and there had been some initial confusion over my lack of baseline scans for comparison, so I assumed we were rehashing that issue again. No, she reiterated emphatically, they found something abnormal on the *new* scan, and I needed *further* testing.

As a nurse, I asked her to read me the radiologist's words, and I found that "abnormal" meant mass, and a good-sized one at that. We calmly planned my follow-up testing, and I hung up the phone...stunned. Was I writing this book for the good of all or did Bob have me doing it for *me*? Suddenly, my world was upside down and I quickly relived the events of my journal but plugged myself into Steve's role. Had Death drawn my card too? So soon? I am not one to overreact, but the thought did cross my mind that my dream of our little tea party might have been a courtesy call...a warning perhaps.

How was I going to tell my husband that he might be writing his own Caring Bridge Journal someday? Yes, I said husband. Remember how I mentioned that God works in mysterious ways? Well, sometimes His plans are farther reaching than any of us can imagine, and one of my anonymous angels turned out to be a very old and dear friend from my past who was put back into my life when I desperately needed some divine intervention.

When I was sixteen and he, Alan, this anonymous angel helper, was nineteen, we became each other's first sweethearts, first loves. We'd met when we were nine and twelve respectively and didn't make the connection until years later when we were sharing childhood pictures of ourselves. We were crazy about each other and spent all our time together—a fact that worried my very strict parents. Soon, my father was encouraging Alan, who was very bright, to go to college and get a degree. Respectful of my father's opinion, Alan followed through and our logistical separation darn near killed us both. We were so lonesome for one another that he bought me a tiny promise ring with little diamonds to demonstrate his intention to return for me.

My father had taken one look at the ring and stated that we were too serious too young, forcing me to return it and end the relationship. Being a dutiful daughter, I reluctantly and tearfully did, but vowed to keep writing Alan. We managed to keep up our correspondence via letters and the occasional long-distance phone call until my father intercepted them and put his foot down, telling me to let the young man finish what he started and for me to concentrate on high school.

Broken-hearted, we both somehow accepted our fate—time and distance carrying us far away from one another. Years passed, we tried to find each other through friends, but there was no Internet or social media to make that easy. Finally, after a good many years had passed, we connected, having married others and raising kids. We were both secretly unhappy but never expressed that to each other; we were instead respectful of each other's situation, so we wished each other well and again lost track of one another.

One day, Alan found me on Facebook, and we were able to chat politely. I had married Steve, and Alan offered his wishes for our happiness. Several years passed when someone pointed out to him that they thought I had brain cancer. He was horrified as my Facebook page said BRAIN CANCER SUCKS followed by a link to my Caring Bridge Journal site. Thinking I was sick, Alan clicked on the link and began to read.

Over the months, he was torn by the sorrow he felt for me and for Steve as well as the desire to do something tangible to help. He feared, however, that any offer would seem an intrusion or appear less than altruistic, so Alan became one of our anonymous angels…the one who sent the carpenter to build the ramp, to fix the drawers and other appliances that had broken, and who paid expenses that we were struggling to meet. We would've never known it was Alan, but after Steve's death, the carpenter had returned to dismantle the ramp only to find out that I had already managed to have it done by one of our firefighter friends. The man had raked his fingers through his hair, a little distressed, while his helper complained, "Mr. Stevens isn't gonna be happy that we didn't get back here in time."

"Mr. Who?" I gasped, suddenly knowing the answer to my question. It all made sense and I placed a call. Alan was annoyed that the men had "outed him" as he never wanted me to feel awkward about his assisting me and had always wanted to be respectful of Steve, but he admitted that he couldn't sit idly by when he knew I was in trouble. No matter what, he had to help…and he had. We ended up talking for a long time about life, family (he'd been raising his daughter on his own for quite a few years), God, and fate, and we agreed that in the future, when I had gotten myself together, I would call, and we'd meet for coffee.

Meanwhile, back at the ranch, my brother Dan and his wife Connie had been privy to the fact that I hadn't had a vacation in three years and probably hadn't had a good night's sleep in almost as long. They also worried that I was facing a tough time when all the well-wishers and helpers faded into the wings, leaving the widow to sit alone in an empty house filled with dust and memories. Therefore, they invited me to join them on a cruise to the Caribbean—my first cruise ever—and I nervously accepted their incredibly generous offer.

Those two events, both gifts from God and given out of kindness—the reconnection with a love from my childhood and the generous offer of a getaway with siblings—proved a double-edged sword that both cut through my grief and cut me off from society. Death, as I said before, sometimes leaves a vacuum that can be filled with all manner of stuff—some lovely and some not, and I was the recipient of both.

What happened next could and might fill another book, but it will suffice to say that on my cruise, I had many hours and endless sea vistas over which to contemplate. I prayed, cried secretly in my cabin, caught up on three years of lost sleep, considered my future, consulted with my brother and sister-in-law, and chatted with a bartender from South Africa who'd lost all his immediate family in a fire, but who had remarried and started again, encouraging me to look at what God can mend. All around me was life and people joyfully living it. At first, I was apprehensive, feeling completely out of place, as if I were in the wrong class just before a test I hadn't studied for, but slowly, I just decided to let it all go…the worry, the fear, the expectations, the preconceived notions, the rules AND the guilt. I decided to laugh and smile.

Then I decided to check my email and found a lovely note from Alan, and I found myself moved to write back. Nothing fancy, just thoughts and impressions. He responded, and before we knew it we were having a marvelous conversation about all the movies, music, books, and things we liked. Amazingly, over the years, we had often selected and appreciated the exact same things and places. We talked about loss too…we'd both experienced that, and we decided that life is short and precious. We also decided that we were adults who could make our own decisions… including sharing lunch.

We did…and more meetings and dates followed—a fact which simply horrified many and nearly scandalized the town. Even those neighbors who saw me daily, knowing that every waking hour of my prior life had been entirely devoted to Steve, and many of our friends and family who knew the depth of our devotion for one another, were so upset that I had begun to converse with my childhood sweetheart that they literally shunned me. It was subtle at first, but one woman confronted me and said she was disgusted with the fact that I was walking daily and losing weight—an affront to my late husband's memory. Most widows, I was briskly informed, recognized at least a year of mourning without cruises or power walks on the boardwalk!

As my excess pounds from three years of sedentary, stress-induced, sleepless living dropped away, so did many of my friends and former supporters. It became very clear who my true friends were and who were the ones who loved to pity a pathetic widow and all the drama that comes with her. I have no doubt that many assumed I had somehow met Alan while Steve was still alive, but no one ever took the time to verify or hear the story—assuming and presuming was much more exciting for them, I suppose… much more fun for them to speculate and gossip.

Ironically, one of my closest and fiercest supporters was and is Steve's daughter, Heather, who knows my heart, my devotion to her dad, and the truth. I suppose that if she, God, Steve, Alan, and I know the truth, then nothing else really matters. So why am I bothering to write this at all? Well, as I said before, my friends, I was going to tell you the good, the bad, and the ugly in the hope that I can be authentic and of help to you.

To hide the truth wouldn't serve anyone who might find him or herself in this position…and I KNOW there are more than a few of you in the complicated aftermath of Death's visit, picking up pieces, trying to put them back together, or throwing them out altogether and starting fresh.

That said, when the doctor called me with the news about my mammogram (you thought I had forgotten about that subject didn't you?) I worried about how to tell my husband, Alan, who was in Washington, DC, prepping a house we owned there for sale. It was almost unbearably lonely to sit down in Florida by myself with such news, but then again, it forced me to feel it and take it to God as I had done so many years ago in that hospital room with Steve. I bundled up that concern, placed it in His lap, and returned to this book, knowing that whichever way things went—it would be okay, because I had met Death many times before, and now we were on speaking terms.

Death Wears High-Tops

Later that night I fell into a deep sleep:

We were back on the porch again sitting knee to knee. Death—or Morty, as he asked to be called—and I. Morty was in his usual robe with his sickle propped against the glass door again, but this time he had on his name tag and a faded old ball cap peeking out from under his hood. He was rocking pleasantly, his black gauzy robe grazing the laces of his new red high-tops, and there was a white T-shirt beneath the robe that hadn't been there before. We rocked in silence as we both watched the dogs run around the pool deck, chasing after lizards.

"I could watch them all day," he finally said, pointing a bony finger toward my Corgis, who took lizard-herding very seriously on their stubby little legs.

"Yep, me too, they LOVE chasing lizards!" I exclaimed. Then I wondered if I should offer my guest a beverage. "Can I get you anything?" I added.

"No, remember last time?" Morty replied.

"Oh yeah." Then suddenly I was apprehensive, because he WASN'T here for tea… Had he pulled my card? Was this MY visit?

He looked at me, tilting his skull to the side, tapping his index finger bone on the arm of the chair.

"What?" I asked, trying to keep my voice calm.

"Oh, nothing really…just wondering." He kept looking at me, unnerving me further.

"Wondering WHAT?"

"Am I REALLY like a turd in a punch bowl?" Oh my gosh, I panicked. Worse than pulling my card, he had read my notes!

"It's just a metaphor," I stammered, "a glimpse of how you COULD be perceived by those who don't understand you."

"Is that how YOU see me?"

I thought for a moment. Here I sit with Death, wearing a ball cap with a HELLO tag and red Converse high-tops, and he is asking me how I see him? Suddenly a flood of memories of brain tumors, coffins, mourners, bagpipes, hospital beds, casseroles, cards, flowers, red wagons, a Blue Moon, and a giant white lap flashed through my mind in an instant. I was for only the briefest second angry, then I confessed.

"Maybe once I saw you that way, but now that I've gotten to know you, you're just a guy—a take-out and delivery guy. A pickup artist. Look, you don't make the orders, you just fill them. You do the best you can with what you're given, and you catch a lot of grief for it—no pun intended. You see it all go down and can't undo any of it. That has to be very difficult for you."

"People think I CAUSE it, you know. They think I cut them down with that (pointing over his shoulder at the scythe), but I only use it to slice the thread that holds their souls to their dead bodies. I mean, who wants to be tied to a dead body for eternity? I harvest them for their next step—it's kind of ceremonial. I see a lot though... unspeakable pain and unimaginable beauty..." He trailed off, lost in unseen memory.

I thought about that...I am sure he did see it all. I wondered what he had seen with us? With Steve? With me? Death must have read my mind.

"Steve was quite a guy. I pulled his card, but it wasn't what I'd expected."

"What do you mean?"

"Well, usually I am told who, when, and where to go, but with Steve I was just told who and where...it said the WHEN card would follow."

"I wonder why," I pondered.

"I did too at first, but I soon figured it out." Death leaned in to make his point. *"Steve's hope and positivity were so powerful that his WHEN was not printed on the card. Let's just say it was negotiable. He was one of the rare ones."* He sat back and rocked vigorously, seemingly pleased to deliver such a compliment.

"Wow..." I was floored.

"And then I watched as his attitude spread like a sickness," his rocking slowed deliberately, *"but it wasn't sick at all—it was wonderful, and soon I found myself hoping I wouldn't have to pull your card or anyone's in your family or your friends or neighbors... It just spread... the love...it just kept spreading."* He stopped mid-rock, lost in thought.

"So, you aren't heartless."

"What? No, look," he responded, pointing to his empty chest, "no heart, but I do have a soul, I guess, because I feel the loved one's pain when I cut the thread, and I know that sometimes people act better when I am around, or just after I leave, and it bothers me when they don't. That is not an easy thing to LIVE with, you know."

We sat silently for another minute or two rocking gently. Then he clapped his bony palms together as if to change the subject. "Anyway, thanks for the help with the whole PR and image thing. I had never really thought about how my approach could make any difference."

It touched me to think that his image mattered to Death, and in that, it gave him meaning, purpose. I could see that he could feel it too and was trying to embrace it. From his red high-tops to his HELLO name tag to his ratty old ball cap. He was trying to give himself a makeover to present himself as more acceptable, approachable, respectable, and maybe even likable. In return, he had made himself vulnerable and therefore…a little bit human.

His coming for Steve had never been personal or an attack at all—he had just been doing his job—an uninvited guest who ended up becoming—strangely enough—a familiar acquaintance and maybe perhaps even a friend. I could see that now.

"So," I ventured, "this is just a friendly visit today? You're not… working?"

"What? NO!" he exclaimed. "No, I just came to thank you for giving me a chance. For having me over before and now for talking me up in your book. I really appreciate it."

"My pleasure." I beamed, and I meant it—perhaps I may live to see it published after all. "Quick question though," and he nodded for me to continue. "I like the new look, Morty, but I'm curious—tell me about the hat—it looks 'seasoned.' Where'd you get it?"

He reflexively reached up, touching the brim, and replied, "Oh, I had a pickup to make—a really nice old guy—a preacher who recognized me right away by my sickle. He wasn't the slightest bit afraid and seemed to want to talk, so he told me he had started out life as a farmer like his daddy before him, using a sickle just like mine to cut down the wheat before his daddy had bought a real tractor. Then he shared that he had left the farm at twenty-one to become a minister because he'd been called to sow a different kind of seed and reap a different kind of harvest if you know what I mean. I asked him how his father had handled it, and he told me:

"'Well, I always thought he was disappointed in me, that I'd left the farm and all, but just before YOU came to get him, he called me to his side and told me he was proud of the work I had done, and then he put his favorite ball cap on my head.'

"I remembered that job," recalled Morty, "and the family standing around the old farmer as he was passing. I could tell he had lived a hard life but was a good man. His son was a lot younger then, and that was a long time ago, but I wanted him to know it mattered, so I told him I remembered. Then the old preacher smiled with a faraway look and touched the brim of his old faded red cap and smiled to himself. 'I guess I won't be needing this anymore where I'm headed.' So, he removed it and held it tenderly, looking at it one last time, and then he did something I wasn't expecting."

"What was that?" I was riveted.

"He handed it to me," said Morty softly, "and he said: 'Here, I want you to have it. This hat has seen a lot of stuff—kinda like you and me, and I guess we both spend all our time focusing on the harvest. I just want you to know I bear you no grudge.'"

"Wow," I marveled, "that is beautiful..."

Morty reverently touched the brim and looked down at his lap, silent.

"I bet it means a lot to you. What does the hat say, Morty? May I see it?"

Morty then proudly, gently, carefully lifted his hood to show me, and if a skull with sockets for eyes and no lips could beam with joy—his did—as I read the faded words:

SOW LOVE, REAP JOY

I think Steve—my farmer turned firefighter, turned angel, and his best buddy, Bob, would wholeheartedly agree.

Parting Support:
What Do I Do with
This Black Hole?

Okay, now that you brave folks have completed my story, you may find *your* story to be quite similar, or it might be very different. I have had many friends who have lost loved ones in a vast variety of ways—all of which were excruciating to them personally, and none of which were deemed easy by any of them. Something we all could agree upon, however, when discussing our personal relationship with Death or the loss of a loved one, was the inevitable and unavoidable Great Empty...the Void...the Vacuum... *The Black Hole* that Death left behind.

When we find ourselves alone, standing in the quiet, after all the mourners, family, neighbors, and friends have walked away, we are left with deafening silence and crushing vacancy, and the strangest sense of *what do I do with this thing I cannot see?* That realization causes instant panic in many of us who are not accustomed to solitude, and we often instinctively perceive it as pain. Even those of us comfortable being alone a lot will feel the pain of that empty space—of that person who will never be there in the flesh as we knew him or her again. So, what do we do with that?

It is said that time heals all wounds, and there is truth to that, but it also can leave disfiguring scars if we're not attentive. Well then, you ask, what *do* we do? We can always start by turning to the experts for help. Here is where the collective wisdom of thousands upon thousands of sages has aligned (that of prophets, gurus, monks, coaches, therapists, and battle-scarred warriors who've slogged through those trenches), and to quote any one of them would be to quote hundreds. The wisdom is so prevalent that it is common knowledge to many—some of us lucky enough to have a guide teaching it to us, the rest of us having to stumble through, picking it up as we go.

My goal here is not to invent something new—that is impossible as this knowledge most likely predates written history. No, my final goal here is to share some universal tenets that I have either stubbed my toe upon in my stagger through grief or have had imparted by those much wiser than I. These gems provide no magic bullets or miracle pills to remove the pain, but they do help restore hope that someday it won't hurt to breathe again.

The Collective Wisdom—

#1—**The Disbelief:** Sometimes it is surreal to find that *you* are now one of *those* people whose loved one is dying or has died. You are finding it hard to imagine life without this person or you may even deny it will ever happen because you're filled with such massive hope for a miraculous recovery (that was me for a while).

Or, you simply cannot believe the news that *you* are now one of *those* people who has just lost a loved one in a tragic, unexpected, sudden way when you were making big plans that very morning. Just know that it is normal and common to be in some measure of denial or disbelief when first encountering Death.

#2—**The Anger**: Sometimes, but not always, you feel ripped off. How could this happen to *me*? To *him*? To *us*? You may blanch at the unfairness of it all as you lose your honor student while the drunk driver survives…or you may bear the shame of being kin to the drunk driver whom everyone reviles (but whom you still love with all your heart). This, too, is normal—I personally call it coming to grips with the truth. If you're not indignant or upset, then perhaps you're not truly acknowledging or seeing the truth that Death has arrived. Anger often tells us that we are alive and human, so go ahead and express it to someone, then *agree to put it down and walk away* or it just may overtake you, clinging like the Swamp Thing, weighing you down with its slimy, smelly, putrid bogginess, pulling you under and eventually suffocating you. Anger is a temporary purgative for limited use ONLY.

* Note: There are some people, however, who have managed—either through multiple encounters with Death or life's challenges, or through deep, abiding faith—to free themselves entirely from the *why me* questions, realizing that everyone faces trials at some point and that tribulation is ubiquitous…but those people are special and few…and blessed.

#3—**The Crying Time(s)**: This is where you *feel* that loss. *Feel* that empty space. *Feel* that vacuum. This is where I sniffed my father's clothing hanging in his closet, or held my husband's pillow, sobbed into the couch wearing his T-shirts, begging him to give me a sign, pouring out my brokenness to God and the angels. In many cultures they rend or tear their clothing, put ashes on their heads, throw themselves on the graves, claw at their own faces, scream and wail, rolling on the ground. That sounds rather cathartic to me. The point of this time is to *feel* the sadness and depression…the pain of the loss. I remember telling my students that stuffing down a painful feeling rather than addressing it was like trying to shove a beach ball under water. The farther under you press it, the harder it is to hold down, and when it finally breaks free (which it always does), it shoots up with a mighty blast and splash, way above the water's surface. Stuffing down grief and *feelings* at this time can have the same effect. They are going to come out somehow, some way. Might as well let them out in the beginning so you can move forward without the beach ball of suppressed emotion smacking you up under the chin later when you're not expecting it.

#4—**The Reasoning Time:** I can recall hearing a grieving widow speak in absolutes a few months after her husband's death. She would *never* have another love again. She would *never* find happiness again. She would *never* find a new home for his things again, and so on. No one troubled her about it as we knew she was grieving, but after a while, it was as if she had declared them so often that she felt to do otherwise would be a betrayal of her love and loyalty to her late spouse. That was when we had to gently help her see that there was still room for happiness. We reminded her that when she had her second child, she didn't love her first one any less. So, maybe, just maybe, loving others wasn't an exclusive proposition. It took a while for reason to set in, but if you find yourself or a loved one caught in the guilt or grief trap, looping back on the "never again" statements, ask him or her if she still loves her kids or if he still loves his brother or if they still love their dog. If the answer is yes, then I encourage you to remind them that love *still* exists and then remind them to channel that pent-up love toward their *living* family and friends or perhaps even in a new, unexplored direction. Love is too precious a commodity to hoard or stifle.

#5—**The Remembering and Honoring Time:** Often when we can stop the tears long enough to admit we still have the capacity to love, we then accept the loss a little more easily. We can even find ways to honor and fondly remember our loved one (which is a gentle release). I found that rather than hearing or talking about what I missed or how upset I was that Steve was gone, his friends and family truly wanted to talk about the *living* part of him. We told funny stories about his sense of humor, his kindness to all the neighbors, his gentleness with nature, his love for flowers and growing things, his witty quips to dispel awkward moments, and his refusal to let others "get to him" by making himself the brunt of the joke, thus earning him universal endearment. As we did that, through writing his Caring Bridge journal while he was dying, and later remembering with friends and family after, I began to focus only on the admirable traits he had, the qualities I loved and wanted to emulate. Soon, I would quietly find myself asking what he would do or how he would handle any given situation, and before I knew it, Steve was no longer a distant concept, a dead husband, a Black Hole of grief I could never fill. He was *there* in a new, healthy, and meaningful way.

#6—**Filling the Black Hole**: Okay, we all know that in space, the gravity of a Black Hole is so dense that it swallows all mass or even light in its general vicinity, growing larger as it does. So, too, is the case with the Black Hole of grief. If we allow it to grow by feeding it all our light, hope, joy, plans, aspirations, relationships, hobbies, and dreams, it will gladly swallow them up and demand more, leaving us in a state of perpetual, unresolved, unhealthy, debilitating sadness. Black Holes are sneaky at first because they know we suffer, which causes us pain, and they use that knowledge to tempt us into finding ways to ignore it, stuff it, or escape it. Then, when we succumb, choosing to avoid the pain as discussed above, we live out the beach ball scenario. We stuff our feelings and aspirations down, then we *lose* control, which often prompts us to throw all sorts of things into the Black Hole in wild desperation to fill it. Sometimes these things seem innocuous, such as cloistering ourselves off from groups to binge-watch a TV series; or wondering who cares anymore if we take a drag off this cigarette even though we quit smoking years ago; or who would notice if we just ate a quart of ice cream for dinner instead of feeding ourselves as we used to; or why shouldn't we treat ourselves to an extra glass of wine each night? The Black Hole is voracious, an *addict*, and whatever you throw at it will *never* serve to fill it. *The Black Hole can never be satisfied!*

Except by one thing.

The Black Hole cannot exist in the presence of *love*. As far as I know they're still working out the mathematics of that, but we just need to know that the concept is true.

Love lasts. I learned that from Death. I learned that from Bob (God). I learned that from Steve, and I learned that from all those people in my life whom I *still* love and who *still* love me. I learned that from my kids, and I learned that from Alan. I even learned that from my two Corgis, who never seem to run out of it.

So, in a nutshell, Death only picks *up* a shell. What we love always remains…and if we want to resurrect it and keep it alive forever, then embody the good, embrace the love, and prime the pump to keep it flowing by sharing it with others. As Death reminded us all, SOW LOVE, REAP JOY. Now get planting!

Final Observation: Raising the Blinds

I have a confession to make. As I was prepping the final copy of this manuscript for the publishing team, I found myself dragging my feet. People began asking questions, making comments, and most of all, questioning my commitment to bring this book to fruition. I had all the pieces in place, the photo releases, certain permissions granted, the grammar corrected, the wording scrutinized, changed, and changed back again. So, what was holding me back? I had no answer. I did a mental checklist to determine whether I was performing an act of self-sabotage or whether I had genuinely lost my nerve for fear of exposing my heart and soul to the critics of the world, offering up my "baby" for them to pick apart or perhaps embrace. In the end, I realized that neither option felt true, so I decided to wait, meditate, and pray for the answer.

As the days went by, I felt calm about the whole thing as others continued their queries. I gave bogus answers, including: "I just need one more signed release before sending off the packet," but my friends and family are far too smart for that nonsense. I should've entrusted them with the truth, but they're reading it now, so the cat's out of the bag. In all honesty, there was something deep within my soul telling me to wait. It wasn't a voice, a winged messenger, or a dream, but rather a quiet and very firm *knowing* that I could not ignore. With each passing day I prayed that some sort of sign would arrive before I forgot what I had written altogether, but there was nothing…and nothing taught me everything.

While waiting for an answer, I was reminded of what I had written in the journal about how Bob (God) answers in His own time but always *in* time, and that we can never always know the *why* of things, but we can always count on these two truths: His love and that Death is *never* the end. Ironically, I received the sign after recently spending a time in dark mourning, blinded by tears of grief—not for myself but for some of my family members who had just lost their beloved baby during childbirth…especially cruel in that it was but another in a series of devastating losses in their immediate family. They're so young, kind, giving, successful, and meaningful to all who know them that it was made painfully clear to me that no one, no matter how good, is exempt from tragedy, but rather is either strengthened *through* or broken *by* it. I am sure they have the grace to grow stronger through their grieving and live to guide others through their own inevitable time in the Valley. That is my fervent prayer for them.

What I want to close with is this small observation that I made as a result. Some time has passed since my *own* time in the Valley, so perhaps I had forgotten the full impact and gut-wrenching agony of such heart-rending news. After the phone call, I found myself brimming with tears for days, lost in thought, forgetting conversations in the middle, failing to be fully present in meetings where people wondered what was wrong with me or if I was simply being indifferent. It brought me back to the darkness that we all share when the Black Hole opens, and my mood was further dampened by the fact that my husband Alan was in one place and I in another for two separate prior commitments. I returned to our empty RV, where we were temporarily encamped on an assignment; the shades were already drawn, it was dark and cave-like, so I hunkered down under the covers with the dogs, calling it an early night. The next morning, the little rascals awakened me *way* before I was ready to rise, only to find my gut churning with sadness and a darkness that I knew all too well. I could feel that old wet blanket of misery and despair creeping up, whispering, "Stay down, do nothing, hide under the covers, and shut out the world. It is all too much to bear today. Maybe you can live tomorrow, but just give up on today." The dogs apparently *did not hear* that voice as they continued to paw at me until I threw on a jacket over my pajamas, staggered out of the RV, and let them do their business. It was cold, and I'd expected that, but I was surprised to find the sun was shining because it had been so dark *inside* that I had mistakenly assumed it was the same *outside* as well.

Without another thought, running on automatic, I immediately raised all the blinds in the entire RV (making it a fishbowl for the neighbors), letting the glorious sunlight beam through every window. Almost at once, as if emotions mirrored actions, I felt my steadily growing Black Hole contract when I gazed beyond my immediate surroundings and took in the greater view. Nothing spectacular, but it was as if Bob were explaining something without saying a word. This is what I saw:

The sun rose, as it always does until our appointed time with Morty. The sky was a riveting blue with a single cloud that reminded me that rain can come, but it doesn't command the day. The live oaks were bowing gracefully, their tufts of Spanish moss waving gently. I studied that for a moment, realizing that I knew a breeze was blowing—not because I could *feel* it—but because I could *see* their movement. Bob is like that too sometimes when I do not feel His comfort and peace directly, but I know it is there through witnessing the goodness of others. As if to ensure I got His message, just then, a neighbor pedaled up to another who was struggling with a ladder as he attempted to take down his Christmas decorations. The first man hopped off his bike and steadied the ladder—who knew where he was headed or if he was postponing something important for himself in the service of another? Soon, the wizened woman who diligently keeps the entrance to the park free of weeds ambled by with her gray-muzzled mutt, both treading carefully but cheerfully down the road—the dog appreciating the smells in the grass, the woman stopping every so often to appreciate her clearly beloved companion.

It was true that I'd cocooned myself away in the snug darkness of my RV for reasons of grief, perhaps depression, and maybe for deep contemplation, and that was okay. However, it wasn't until I raised the blinds that had been *blinding* me and gazed *through* the glass and *beyond* that I could see that life was still happening. This time, instead of resenting it, however, or feeling as if it was somehow disrespectful of the tragedy that had befallen my family, I looked at things through older and wiser eyes. The fact that life goes on is a good thing. It reassures us that life will again be there for us when we're ready to re-engage. It means that there are those who are still alive to help us in our time of distress, and it reminds us that we are all transient beings— "spiritual beings having a human experience" (to quote Dr. Wayne Dyer). I know with all my heart that I will see and embrace my lost loved ones again, so I simply need to learn patience and to appreciate those who live, love, and surround me *today*.

I had awakened in darkness—brooding, lonely, grieving—feeling the makings of a new Black Hole that threatened to swallow what happiness I had found, but I had decided to turn it over to Bob, counting on the promised comfort of the Holy Spirit. Nothing of biblical proportions happened…but then again, not all miracles need to be huge to be fantastic. I placed my bundle of pain in the Master's lap, and I was simply told to OPEN THE BLINDS…and by doing so, this blind, stubborn, often foolish woman could finally see the truth that nothing we love ever really dies. It's time now to finish this book, step out, and go live.

Until we meet again, Bob bless you.

Jan Briddell Stevens, RN, CCH would love to hear from you!

Please feel free to share your personal stories of getting to know Death with Jan, or if you would like to have Jan come to your organization or corporation to discuss dealing with grief, loss, and moving on, contact her at:

JanBriddellStevens@gmail.com

She would also be happy to offer seminars and or workshops for all age groups and enjoys speaking to large groups in a keynote capacity, bringing humor and levity to the most difficult of subjects. Hypnotherapy is an integral part of her work and can be an effective tool for those caught in the grief cycle.

If you or anyone you know seems stuck in grief and unable to move beyond loss, please feel free to reach out. Remember, you're never truly alone.

Also, if you enjoyed this book – if it made you cry, laugh, shake your fist at Death or see him in a new light – then PLEASE leave a review on Amazon or the website of the store from where you purchased it…each review brings us one step closer to sponsorship of further publication copies that can be provided to those who are hurting and in need of hope.

Many humble thanks,
Jan Briddell Stevens

CPSIA information can be obtained
at www.ICGtesting.com
Printed in the USA
LVHW03s0901230718
584632LV00009B/406/P